ORPHAN TRAINS TO MISSOURI

Project Sponsors
Missouri Center for the Book, Jefferson City
Western Historical Manuscript Collection,
University of Missouri–Columbia

Consultant
Donald M. Lance

Special Thanks
Susanna Alexander
A. E. Schroeder
Paul Szopa, Academic Support Center,
University of Missouri–Columbia
State Historical Society of Missouri, Columbia

Missouri Heritage Readers

General Editor,
REBECCA B. SCHROEDER

Each Missouri Heritage Reader explores a particular aspect of the state's rich cultural heritage. Focusing on people, places, historical events, and the details of daily life, these books illustrate the ways in which people from all parts of the world contributed to the development of the state and the region. The books incorporate documentary and oral history, folklore, and informal literature in a way that makes these resources accessible to all Missourians.

Intended primarily for adult new readers, these books will also be invaluable to readers of all ages interested in the cultural and social history of Missouri.

Books in the Series

Food in Missouri: A Cultural Stew,
by Madeline Matson

Jesse James and the Civil War in Missouri,
by Robert L. Dyer

On Shaky Ground: The New Madrid Earthquakes of 1811–1812,
by Norma Hayes Bagnall

Orphan Trains to Missouri,
by Michael D. Patrick and Evelyn Goodrich Trickel

The Osage in Missouri,
by Kristie C. Wolferman

Paris, Tightwad, and Peculiar: Missouri Place Names,
by Margot Ford McMillen

The Trail of Tears across Missouri,
by Joan Gilbert

ORPHAN TRAINS TO MISSOURI

MICHAEL D. PATRICK
EVELYN GOODRICH TRICKEL

UNIVERSITY OF MISSOURI PRESS
COLUMBIA AND LONDON

University of Missouri Press, Columbia, Missouri 65201
Printed and bound in the United States of America

Library of Congress Cataloging-in-Publication Data

Patrick, Michael, 1935–
Orphan trains to Missouri / Michael D. Patrick, Evelyn Goodrich Trickel.
p. cm.—(Missouri heritage readers)
Includes bibliographical references and index.
Summary: Discusses the use of orphan trains to place orphaned or abandoned children in homes in nineteenth-century Missouri.
ISBN 0-8262-1121-6 (pbk. : alk. paper)
1. Orphan trains—Juvenile literature. 2. Orphans—New York (State)—New York—Juvenile literature. 3. Abandoned children—New York (State)—New York—Juvenile literature. 4. Adoptees—Missouri—Juvenile literature. 5. Children's Aid Society (New York, N.Y.)—History—Juvenile literature. [1. Orphan trains. 2. Orphans.] I. Trickel, Evelyn, 1932– . II. Title. III. Series.
HV985.P39 1997
362.73'4'0973—dc21 97-12244
CIP
AC

∞™ This paper meets the requirements of the American National Standard for Permanence of Paper for Printed Library Materials, Z39.48, 1984.

Designer: Stephanie Foley
Typesetter: BOOKCOMP
Printer and Binder: Thomson-Shore, Inc.
Typefaces: Cargo and Palatino

For all those who rode the orphan trains to Missouri

CONTENTS

PREFACE

Evelyn Sheets and Evelyn Trickel of Trenton became known as "the Evelyns" throughout Missouri in the 1980s. They jointly made slide presentations on such topics as "Grundy County History in Stone," "A Place Called Poosey," and "Up and Down Bound in Missouri River Steamboats, 1819–1900." Their programs were seen by hundreds of people throughout the state.

While teaching an adult class in genealogy in Trenton, Evelyn Sheets discovered that many survivors of the orphan trains lived in Missouri. She and Evelyn Trickel began interviewing them, and from these interviews they developed another slide presentation. Each time they presented it, they found additional orphan-train survivors and their descendants to interview.

They asked me to join them in working on a research grant from the Missouri Humanities Council. Soon we were interviewing even more people from all corners of the state about the orphans who came west on the trains.

The names of the Reverend J. W. and Mrs. Swan, the chaperons on many orphan trains, kept coming up in interviews. It was the work of the Swans that first inspired us to continue our search for orphan-train children. We thought of their dedication to their work and the difficulties they faced in bringing trainloads of children to Missouri.

We also thought of the emotions they must have felt when they had to separate brothers and sisters from the same family or remove children from their new homes. For them the work must have been both rewarding and heartrending.

These thoughts and questions led us to hold a reunion in Trenton on Labor Day weekend 1985 for those who had ridden the trains and their descendants. So many people came and enjoyed it that Trenton and other towns now have annual reunions.

At those early reunions the orphan trains came vividly alive again. The opportunity to talk with a few of those who rode the trains or with the children and grandchildren of others gave us an understanding of the impact the trains had on the lives of all Missourians.

The histories of people who had endured emotional and physical hardships in coming to Missouri as children became very personal for us. Each of the orphan-train riders we talked with seemed to have a courageous spirit earned at an early age. Their willingness to talk about their lives made us realize that they had long ago dealt with the emotional wounds the experience of the trains had caused them.

The orphans, their children, grandchildren, and other descendants seem to have learned to deal with life bravely and without complaint. As Rose Cranor, who had been separated from her brother more than seventy years earlier, said at the reunion in Trenton, "You have to deal with life as you find it."

The Evelyns asked me to join them in writing a book about the orphans. All three of us realized that the orphan-train riders and their sons, daughters, and grandchildren had an important story that should be told.

The book was progressing well when Evelyn Sheets was struck by a car in 1986. She was critically injured in the accident and remained in a coma for more than three years. She died on June 16, 1989.

Evelyn Trickel and I carried on our project without her, but we never forget that she was the one who first started us interviewing, researching, and writing about the orphan trains to Missouri.

As a teacher of adults at Trenton College and as a student of Missouri folklore and culture, we feel sure that Evelyn Sheets would be proud that her work became a part of the Missouri Heritage Readers Series of the University of Missouri Press.

—*Michael Patrick*

ACKNOWLEDGMENTS

First, our thanks go to the orphan-train riders and their families who shared their memories and family pictures with us.

We would also like to thank the librarians and archivists who helped us search for documentary and photographic materials and answered our many inquiries. Fae Sotham at the State Historical Society of Missouri in Columbia, Cindy Stewart of the University of Missouri Western Historical Manuscript Collection–Columbia, and D. J. Diciacca of the University Archives guided us to many photographs.

Mr. Victor Remer, archivist at the Children's Aid Society in New York, and staffs at the Museum of the City of New York, the University of Maryland Baltimore County, and the Kansas Historical Society provided information and materials not available in Missouri.

Orphan Trains to Missouri could not have been written without the pioneering work of Evelyn Sheets, who started interviewing orphan-train survivors and their families more than a decade ago, recording their stories for future researchers.

Additionally, Michael Patrick received invaluable help from the staff of the University of South Alabama Baldwin County in the final stages of writing this book.

INTRODUCTION

Many citizens of the United States take pride in the fact that their country is a nation of immigrants. They believe that the United States of the nineteenth and early twentieth centuries offered opportunities for every newcomer. Early immigration laws encouraged the poor of Europe to find new hope and start new lives in the United States. "Give me your tired, your poor, your huddled masses": these lines on the Statue of Liberty remind us of this time in U.S. immigration history.

Many believed the United States would become a kind of melting pot. New citizens were expected to "melt" into the mainstream of society and work to become prosperous members of their communities. This sometimes happened, but, in truth, the immigrants often exchanged a bad situation in their native country for an even worse one on the streets of New York and other industrial cities.

Historians have noted that there were at least three distinct stages of mass migration to the United States during the nineteenth century. Many of these immigrants were people who had lost hope in the future because of poverty, religious oppression, political upheaval, or war in their native countries.

The stage of immigration from 1830 to 1860 is usually called "the Celtic period." Most of the immigrants at that time were from Ireland, the Scottish Highlands, and Wales. But many also came from the Upper Rhine valley and adjoining districts of Germany. Most of the Celts and many of the Germans came because of economic hardships in their native homelands.

The Irish potato famine of the 1840s and uncaring absentee landlords were very important reasons for mass migration by the Irish. During the potato famine 1 million of the Irish people starved to death, and 3 to 4 million Irish emigrated to Canada, Australia, New Zealand, and the United States. Famine and absentee landlords who charged high rent on their land reduced the population of Ireland from 8 million to 3 million in one decade.

There were crop failures in Germany also. In addition, German immigrants wanted to escape heavy taxes at home and gain religious freedom. Immigrants from every country hoped for better lives for their children.

The second wave of immigration, from 1860 to 1890, brought more Celts and Germans to the United States. The largest number of Scandinavian immigrants also arrived during these years.

Migration from German-speaking countries continued in the third stage, from 1890 to 1914. But the largest groups during this period were immigrants from Slavic countries and from several countries around the Mediterranean Sea.

It is estimated that during these three stages of mass migration, some 35 million people left their countries to come to the United States.

An important reason for this mass migration was the attraction of free or inexpensive land in the western United States. In fact, a nineteenth-century broadside song promised farms for all who came:

> Come along, come along, make no delay
> Come from every nation; Come from every way
> Our land is broad enough—don't be alarmed,
> For Uncle Sam is rich enough to give us all a farm.
> (from "Uncle Sam's Farm," H. De Marsan broadside)

Some German immigrants did find rich farmland in the United States. The Missouri River valley was one of the areas where many German immigrants settled to farm. The Germans also established towns such as Hermann, Freeburg, Westphalia, and Rich Fountain in Missouri.

"Irish Emigrants Leaving Home." The Irish famine of the 1840s, known as "the Great Hunger," and the troubles that followed caused a mass Irish emigration to the United States. The song "The Green Fields of America" promised that a newcomer in America could "in peace and comfort" spend his life and "never know misery or strife." (State Historical Society of Missouri, Columbia)

A popular nineteenth-century song in Ireland, "The Green Fields of America," glorified the opportunities available in the United States. But instead of settling in farmland areas, many Irish immigrants settled in the cities of Boston and New York. Some found work in the factories. Others, especially Irish women, worked as servants for the rich.

Many Irishmen worked as laborers, building the railroads as they progressed westward. Often they lived in "Irish shanties" along the tracks. These shanties could be taken down and rebuilt farther down the tracks for the next job. In fact, much of the lumber for Henry David Thoreau's cabin at Walden Pond, built near Concord, Massachusetts, in 1845, had originally been part of an Irish shanty. Some people in the eastern United States came to know the distinction between the shanty Irish (the poor) and the lace-curtain Irish (the well-to-do).

Some Irish immigrants did find opportunities in the Midwest. In fact, there were so many Irish immigrants in

St. Louis that an area in the south part of that city is still known as "the Kerry Patch," named for a county in Ireland. Father John Hogan of St. Louis tried to establish a settlement of Irish immigrants in the Missouri Ozarks, but during the Civil War the settlers were in a no-man's-land, caught between Union and Confederate soldiers and raided by bushwhackers. By the time the war ended the immigrants were gone, and even today it is not clear what happened to them. However, the area of Mark Twain National Forest near Doniphan is still known as the "Irish Wilderness."

Italian immigrants also came to Missouri during the nineteenth and early twentieth centuries. The central part of St. Louis known as "the Hill" is still mostly populated by people of Italian descent. Other Italian immigrants settled in Phelps County, Missouri, near the town of St. James, and established vineyards, wineries, and a town named Rosati.

In Willa Cather's story "Neighbor Rosicky," a Slavic immigrant described the poverty he had experienced in Europe. Newspaper articles had told him of prosperous Czech farming communities in the U.S. West, and he had longed to go there. He arrived in New York City and worked as a tailor, but he soon found New York City just as stifling as European cities. "It struck young Rosicky that this was the trouble with big cities; they built you from the earth itself, cemented you away from any contact with the ground." For Rosicky, and for many Slavic, German, Italian, and Irish immigrants like him, the Midwest promised freedom and opportunity.

But often the immigrants did not have enough money to get to the Midwest where land was available. And many did not have the practical skills necessary to become homesteaders. With the industrial expansion of the United States, European immigrants in many cases settled in eastern manufacturing cities where there was work. They usually lived in neighborhoods with people from their own country and kept their own language and customs. These immigrants provided an abundant, cheap source of labor for U.S. factories of the late nineteenth century.

Rapid urban growth led to the development of ethnic neighborhoods in the cities. New York City was formed culturally and divided geographically by its national and ethnic groups. As early as 1830 the area known as "Five Points" in New York was populated mostly by Irish immigrants. By the next generation the Irish area covered almost the entire Lower East Side. Because of overcrowding and poverty, the Bowery, a section of Lower Manhattan that had been the theater district, began to earn its reputation as a rough, dangerous place.

As the Irish kept coming to U.S. cities, they were often greeted with signs that read "Help Wanted. No Irish Need Apply." Comic songs mocked Irish customs and often depicted Irishmen drinking and fighting. Phrases such as "the fighting Irish" or an "Irish temper" are still heard today, but during the heavy nineteenth-century immigration there were many jokes mocking the Irish. Potatoes were called "Irish apricots," and the wheelbarrow was called an "Irish chariot." Some people joked that the wheelbarrow was a great invention because it had helped the Irish learn to walk on their "hind legs."

By 1850 the German area of New York City, just north of the Irish district, was called "Kleindeutschland" (Little Germany). It extended from the Bowery to the tenth, eleventh, and thirteenth wards, or electoral districts. Germans, too, were mocked for their accents, food customs, and drinking habits. A comic song, "Sourkrout and Sausages" was sung by a Mr. S. Barry at the Bowery Theatre to "thunders of applause." The songwriter imitated a German accent, and the chorus named some favorite German foods and drink: "Sourkrout un Sausages / Schnapps un lager beer."

Soon Italian immigrants established Little Italy on the Lower East Side. There, like other immigrants, they kept their food customs, and at the turn of the century a social worker complained that a family was "Not yet Americanized. Still eating Italian food." People sang songs such as "Down in Spaghetti Row," and garlic was often called "Italian perfume."

These waves of immigrants from Europe provided U.S. factories with cheap labor. They were paid as little as possible for their work and lived in run-down apartment buildings called tenements. New York City, as a major port of entry for the three great waves of nineteenth-century immigration, soon filled all of its available housing.

More than 1.2 million poor people lived in crowded tenements in New York City by the late nineteenth century. When these buildings filled up, thousands of people had no choice except to live in the streets, under steps, beneath bridges, or in open lots and fields.

Crowds of children that the police called "street arabs" filled the alleys and sidewalks of New York City. Some of these children had been abandoned by their parents. Some had left their homes to escape the abuse of their parents and to hunt for food and shelter. On the streets, they lived a hand-to-mouth existence and depended on their wits to avoid the police and social workers. Some were orphans and had no other way to live except through street crime and begging.

Even when new immigrants succeeded in finding work and living space for their families in the cities, life in the United States was hard. Workers did not have the protection of government agencies or labor unions. Injuries could prevent them from working for long periods of time or permanently disable them. They had no sick leave. There was no disability insurance. They faced frequent layoffs. Because there were more workers than there were jobs, wages were frequently reduced below living costs for many immigrants.

Even those who established themselves in the workforce could not always support their children. Many children added to the family income by whatever poor wages they could earn selling newspapers, shining shoes, or selling

"Immigrants Landing, New York." Immigrants often arrived in the United States without the resources to care for their families. A historian reports that the average Italian immigrant brought $12.67 with him. Jacob A. Riis, a Danish writer and photographer, estimated that more than 95 percent of the people living in New York tenements were foreign born. (State Historical Society of Missouri, Columbia)

matches on the street corners. Many children became pickpockets, purse snatchers, and shoplifters when they could not find work on the streets. Others ran errands for gamblers. Often both girls and boys were forced into prostitution.

The living conditions on the streets of the United States' richest city were filthy and dangerous. An unpublished manuscript of a social worker in the archives of the Children's Aid Society of New York described sewage floating in the gutters. The odors caused by filth and lack of sanitation overflowed from the apartment buildings onto the streets. Garbage was everywhere.

Men crippled from industrial accidents or too old to work survived by begging and petty thievery. Men and women,

"Street Arabs—Night Boys in Sleeping Quarters." Children who had no homes roamed the streets during the day and often had to sleep in alleys and doorways at night. (Jacob A. Riis photo, Library of Congress)

destroyed by alcohol or drugs, slept in gutters and stole to have enough money to feed their addictions. Women with venereal diseases sold themselves openly, day and night. Thieves, thugs, and sexual predators roamed the alleys. The area on the Lower East Side became known as Hell's Kitchen. All New Yorkers, rich and poor, agreed that it was a fitting name.

There were no bathhouses or laundry facilities for poor children. To take baths in the summer, these so-called street arabs could swim in the East River or turn on fire hydrants when the police were not looking. In the winter, they had no place to bathe or launder their clothing. Most had only the clothes they wore. Social workers did what they could but knew of no way to remove homeless children from the streets.

Life on the streets cut these children off from their families and society. Many New York citizens blamed them for street

"Street Arabs in an Areaway of Mulberry Street." Once a pathway lined with mulberry trees, Mulberry Street was nicknamed "Death's Thoroughfare." It was "the foul core of the New York slums." (Jacob A. Riis Collection, Museum of the City of New York)

crime and violence and wanted them placed in orphan homes or prisons. For most of the street arabs, their lives followed a cycle, from loss of contact with their families, to living in the open on the streets, to crime and imprisonment. Well-to-do New York citizens considered them part of the "dangerous classes" who would become worse criminals as adults and be a further threat to society.

One of the wealthy New Yorkers who became concerned about the children was Charles Loring Brace. He had been educated for the clergy and ordained as a Methodist minister. At twenty-six he thought that he did not have the voice, theological knowledge, or ability to preach. In 1853, along with other well-to-do men in New York City, he founded the Children's Aid Society of New York.

The society planned to give food, lodging, and clothing to the street arabs and to provide educational and trade opportunities for them. But the number of children who needed help was so large that it was impossible to care for them all. Brace soon developed a plan to send many of the children to the rural Midwest by train to be placed as foster children with families on farms and in small towns.

Researchers have estimated that from 150,000 to 400,000 children were sent out on what came to be known as "the orphan trains." Perhaps as many as 100,000 were placed in Missouri.

ONE

Charles Loring Brace and the "Street Arabs"

Charles Loring Brace did not fully understand the problems of the street children of the 1850s. He had great faith in the saving grace of education and work, and he first attempted to help the street arabs by offering schooling to prepare them for work.

Through the Children's Aid Society he established industrial schools to give the children skills that would make them useful members of society. In some instances, these schools were successful. But usually attendance was poor, and only a limited number of children learned a useful trade.

Brace also believed that Sabbath-day or Sunday lectures to the young would change the course of their lives. Personal experience soon showed him that most lectures had little effect on the street arabs. When, and if, they did come to hear these Sunday lessons, they were often rowdy, profane, and irreverent.

Not many of these children fit the mold of the heroes in the Horatio Alger stories. Alger, a friend of Brace, was just starting his "rags to riches" novels. One of his most popular novels was *Ragged Dick; or, Street Life in New York with the Boot-Blacks,* first published in 1867 as a serial. *Ragged Dick* was based on the theory that the struggle against poverty and temptation would lead boys to wealth and fame. Alger lived in one of the Children's Aid Society boardinghouses for newsboys and had firsthand experience with the boys' problems. Still, he created an idealized view of their lives and morality in his sentimental novels.

A more realistic view of the newsboys was presented in a popular folk song of the period, "Jimmie Brown, the Newsboy." "Jimmie Brown" tells in vivid terms the street arabs' living conditions:

> My clothes are torn and thin;
> I wander about from place to place,
> My daily bread to win.
> I sell the morning papers, sir,
> My name is Jimmie Brown;
> Most everybody knows I am
> The newsboy of the town.

Just as the song states, most of the children were cold and hungry, wearing thin clothing, and wandering about town. They started before daybreak to sell the morning edition of newspapers and worked until they sold them all. Then they continued selling the afternoon and evening editions. Cities such as New York had many competing daily newspapers, and each paper had several editions every day.

Since newspapers were the primary source for news then, extra editions were often published to get breaking news to the public. To sell these "extras," as they were called, newsboys had to be on call all day and into the evening.

They worked twelve to fourteen hours a day, six days a week. The seventh day they worked fewer hours but only because most papers published only one edition on Sunday unless a major news event caused them to publish an extra.

The newsboys made a profit of a penny or less for every paper sold. Each newsboy had to establish his own selling territory, a street corner, and defend it against all comers. Often fistfights among the boys broke out over the busiest corners.

Their working conditions and living standards were so bleak that in 1899 a group of newsboys organized a strike

"Didn't Live Nowhere." Jacob Riis, who arrived in New York from Denmark "homeless and pennyless" wrote: "Our country has grown great—our cities wealthy—but in their slums lurk poverty and bitterness—bitterness because the promise has not been kept that every man should have an even chance to start well." (Jacob A. Riis Collection, Museum of the City of New York)

against the most powerful newspaper owners in New York, Joseph Pulitzer and William Randolph Hearst. The strike had little impact on the working conditions, but it did make some New Yorkers more aware of the hard lives of the boys.

For entertainment, many of the newsboys attended the Sunday "Boys' Meetings" of the Children's Aid Society. Brace described with good humor the experiences he and others had in delivering moral lectures to these rowdy children.

Sometimes the speakers were met with showers of stones from the street. Sometimes there was a general free-for-all to decide who would get to sit on the benches. At times adult visitors and missionaries were pelted with rocks and garbage by gangs or enemies of those boys who did attend the meetings.

Newsboys worked long hours and earned a penny or less for each paper sold. (Photography Collections, University of Maryland Baltimore County)

But Brace developed some understanding and great affection for these children, especially the newsboys. He saw in them a love of life and a quick sense of humor. This, for him, made them well worth saving from the hardships of the street. To Brace, their good-natured misbehavior only reflected their energy and quick wit.

He enjoyed their humorous and realistic replies to some of the preachers, who, in the course of their Sunday school lessons, tried to question the boys.

One minister asked, "In this parable, my dear boys, of the Pharisee and the publican, what is meant by the 'publican'?"

Quickly, one of the boys in the audience replied, "Alderman, sire, wot keeps a pothouse!" (An alderman was a city official; a pothouse was a pub or tavern.)

Or, the minister asked, "My boys, what is the great end of man? When is he happiest? How would you feel happiest?"

The answer from the boys: "When we'd plenty of hard cash, sir!"

Or, "My dear boys, when your father and your mother forsake you, who will take you up?"

The answer: "The Purlice [police], sir (very seriously). The purlice."

Brace could understand the boys' restless energy and humor. But, he believed, "ungoverned, prematurely sharp, and accustomed to all vileness" as these boys were, "words which came forth from the depths of a man's or woman's heart would always touch some hidden chord."

He thought the homeless boys always had a rather good time. They could enjoy the pleasure of wandering the streets, living by their wits, and experiencing freedom from adult supervision.

The street girls were entirely another matter to Brace, especially when they were involved in prostitution. His attitude about the differences between the sexes reflects the beliefs of the day. For him, girls were by nature more pure than boys. The sexual experiences of boys did not degrade them. But girls were forever ruined by such experiences. He also believed that boys were able to live their free lives on the street without damaging their personalities. Girls, on the other hand, were destroyed emotionally by street life and were exploited if they returned to the street.

Brace and the other members of the Children's Aid Society recognized that even the most upstanding boys and girls faced crime, immorality, and temptation on the streets every day. Because of this, the society set out to get them off the streets and into homes.

One of the first efforts of the society was the lodging house for newsboys. In the beginning the boys regarded this plan with "some suspicion and much contempt." They thought the lodging house was an attempt to make them go to Sunday school. They suspected the superintendent, C. C. Tracy, of being a street preacher. Actually, Tracy was a carpenter.

Charles Loring Brace hoped to help street children. He founded the Children's Aid Society in 1853 and served as its secretary until his death in 1890. The society began the orphan-train movement as a way of taking children out of the poverty of the city. Trainloads of children traveled west for seventy years. (Children's Aid Society, New York)

At first some of them planned to destroy the lodging house. However, the boys soon gave up that plan. They realized a good bed for six cents and a supper for four cents were worth listening to some religious lectures.

The next step in providing for the newsboys was a plan to let them work during the day and go to school in the evening. The society wanted to avoid competition with the public schools, even though the children generally dodged attending school.

At the lodging house for boys, C. C. Tracy introduced Sunday school in a casual manner. After the boys had been impressed by a public funeral, Tracy suggested that they listen to him read from the Bible.

Soon they were discussing the miraculous stories Tracy had read to them. The boys decided Christ was like them in his homelessness. Singing hymns gave them more religious instruction than anything else. They entered into it with gusto. They liked singing songs that seemed very personal to them, such as "There's a Rest for the Weary" and "There's a Light in the Window."

Brace and his associates in the Children's Aid Society were always men of their time, the nineteenth century. For them the strongest moral and spiritual teachings came in the lessons of capitalism.

The newsboys told a folktale among themselves about a news-seller who had become rich through gambling on policy tickets or the numbers game. "Policy" was taken from an Italian word, and policy tickets were used for a form of gambling. The game was popular among the poor and newsboys because they could buy a ticket for ten cents or less. To overcome the boys' faith in gambling, the lodging house established a savings bank, which paid a "rather high rate of interest."

Brace believed this gave them "the 'sense of property,' and the desire for accumulation, which economists tell us, is the basis of all civilization." He did have to admit that such moral lessons in capitalism never completely ended gambling. The boys continued to buy policy tickets. The folklore of the streets still influenced much of what they did.

Elaborate schemes to teach capitalism and moral lessons were not provided for the street girls, however. Brace believed that their problems could be solved by industrial schools. He believed that many of the girls were ashamed to go to public schools because of their ragged clothes. All they needed to overcome their poverty and vices, if they had not already become prostitutes, was to experience the dignity, dress, and morality of the upper-class ladies who taught them.

He wrote of the effect these volunteer, well-to-do teachers had on the street girls: "As these ladies, many of them of remarkable character and culture, began to show the fruits of high civilization to these poor little barbarians, the thought seemed to strike them—though hardly capable of being expressed—that here was a goodness and piety they had never known or conceived."

Brace's optimism is evident throughout his writings. His simple approach to solving the problems of street girls reflects this hopefulness at its height. The homeless boys and girls of the New York streets had problems too complicated to be solved by schools and lodging houses alone.

Nevertheless, during its first year, 1853, the main effort of the Children's Aid Society was to get the children off the streets and into homes and industrial schools. By 1854 thousands of street arabs had filled the facilities of the society to capacity. The board of directors of the society had assumed that they would be receiving only children without parents. They learned quickly that many problems caused children to need aid.

More often than not, the children still had at least one living parent who could not support the family. Under these conditions, sometimes a single child was taken from his or her brothers and sisters and placed in an orphan home.

In still other cases, a father whose wife had died or left him could not care for the children and work too, so he would place the child or children in an orphanage. Widows and abandoned wives had to make similar hard choices about their children.

Probably, many parents of both sexes intended to remove their children from the orphan homes when they could take care of them. In most cases, this did not happen. Often the children never saw their parents again.

Illegitimate and abandoned children presented a different problem. Newborn babies were left on doorsteps or sidewalks. An estimated thirty thousand children were abandoned on the streets of New York City in 1854 alone. Enough orphan homes, lodging houses, schools, and foster homes could not be found or built for all of them.

One year after the establishment of the Children's Aid Society, Brace realized that he had to develop a plan to lessen the overcrowded conditions in the orphanages, lodging houses, and foster homes in New York. The plan that he presented to the board of the society was radical but not new.

Transporting orphans to new geographic areas for placement has been practiced from earliest times to the twentieth century. Ancient Greeks, Jews, and Christians followed such practices. The early Greeks transported infants in large earthenware vessels to a distant temple, where adoptive parents could claim them. In early Jewish history, cities of refuge were established for orphans and others who needed protection. Jewish law allowed a father to indenture or hire out his children to pay debts. Early Christians transported children to isolated communities to protect them from Roman persecution.

The British have used transportation to other countries as a way of taking care of children throughout their history, particularly in the nineteenth and twentieth centuries. Homeless children were sent from England to Canada from 1867 to 1914. During World War II, because of the bombings, children were temporarily placed in the United States and Canada. After the war, thousands of homeless English children were sent to Australia.

The indenture system of England, which was also used in the American colonies, was a method of caring for children who had no parents. For example, four orphans from a poorhouse in London were aboard the *Mayflower* when it landed in 1620. Only one survived the first winter in the Plymouth Colony.

The indenture was a contract that required the child to work as a servant for the adult who had paid for his transportation to the colonies. The system continued after the Revolutionary War. In 1814, Matilda Roberts of New Madrid, in the Missouri Territory, could not write her name. Still, by making her mark on the contract, she indentured her five-year-old son to Bernard Laffout "to be taught the occupation of a farmer." The contract required William Roberts to work for Laffout until the boy's twenty-first birthday, on March 7, 1830.

In addition to teaching the five-year-old boy farming, Laffout was to arrange for Roberts to be taught "to spell, read and write well and to cypher as far as the double rule of three." He was also to provide the boy with "sufficient meat, drink, clothing, lodging, and other necessary things fit and convenient."

If young Roberts completed this sixteen-year contract, Laffout would provide him with "two suits of good wearing apparel, . . . a good young riding horse worth sixty dollars, a good new man's saddle and bridle." William Roberts then would be free to make his own way in the world.

The apprenticeship system was also brought to the United States from Europe. Very young children worked in the trades from the beginning of U.S. history. As an apprentice the child was required by contract to work while learning the skills of a trade from a master carpenter, baker, blacksmith, shoemaker, or other tradesman. This system continued into the industrial age.

Children as young as six or seven were apprenticed to work in factories and mines, often in unsafe and dangerous places. Young girls had fingers small enough to thread bobbins in textile factories. Small boys could dig coal in places too narrow for adult miners. They worked twelve to fourteen hours a day, six days a week. Their only day off was Sunday. Their only holiday was Christmas. There were few child-labor laws to protect them from abusive factory and mine owners.

In both the indenture and the apprenticeship systems, a child had few rights until he or she had fulfilled the terms of the contract, which usually took seven or more years. Charles Brace, however, did not want the children of the orphan trains to be indentured servants or apprentices. To him, this was too much like the involuntary servitude that abolitionists were fighting in 1853.

He learned of the work of the Children's Mission of Boston from J. E. Williams, a former Boston banker and a founding member of the Children's Aid Society of New York. The Boston organization had been transporting orphans throughout New England and the Midwest since 1850.

Brace's plan for orphan trains became much larger than the Boston effort, involving more children and more trains. He believed that the Children's Aid Society had to take quick action to get more than thirty thousand children off the streets of New York as soon as possible. But he wanted the children he planned to send to the Midwest to become members of the families who took them. He did not want them to be house servants or hired hands on farms. The society expected the children placed outside New York City to work in exchange for room, board, and education while being accepted as family members.

The society rejected the practices of the indenture and apprenticeship systems that gave total control of the children to the adults who took them. Under Brace's system, the Children's Aid Society could break the contract at any time if the foster parents did not meet their obligations.

Brace was convinced that the children of the streets would have many benefits in the rural United States. He based his plan on three tenets of American faith: opportunity, hard work, and education. In 1854 he persuaded the board of the society to send the first trainload of orphans west. With this, the orphan trains of the Children's Aid Society of New York were born.

TWO

The Orphan-Train Plan

Charles Loring Brace's vision of rural life, especially that on farms in the West was a romantic one:

> In every American community, especially in a western one, there are many spare places at the table of life. There is no harassing struggle for existence. They have enough for themselves and the stranger too. Those who are able, pay the fares of the children, or otherwise make some gift to the Society, and a little band of young wayfarers and homeless rovers in the world find themselves in comfortable and kind homes, with all the boundless advantages and opportunities of the western farmer's life about them.

As his statement shows, Brace had little understanding of the lives of farmers. Most western families did have "harassing" struggles for existence. And many western farmers thought the young boys and girls on the trains could help relieve some of their struggles by providing more hands for hard physical labor.

Farming at that time was very labor-intensive. Milking was done by hand, not by milking machines. Hogs, cattle, and chickens had to be fed and watered by hand every day. Fields were plowed with mules, horses, and oxen. Corn and other crops were harvested by farm workers, not machines. Even with crops that were harvested with machinery, such as wheat with a reaper, someone had to drive the team of horses pulling the harvesting machine.

Farm animals had to be fed in winter weather, and children were expected to help. (State Historical Society of Missouri, Columbia)

Not much cash was available to pay hired help. Farm workers were often paid in room and board and produce. Surplus milk, eggs, livestock, and crops were bartered at the general store for staples, shoes, and sometimes "yard goods," fabric sold by the yard for homemade clothing.

Often any cash the farmer received at harvest time was saved to start the next year's crops. The term *seed money* was first used by farmers who had only enough cash from the fall harvest to buy seeds for planting in the spring or who sometimes had to borrow "seed money" from the bank.

Every hand was needed, and all farm children had daily chores to do, seven days a week. Both boys and girls gathered eggs, milked the cows in the morning and at night, fed and watered the livestock every day, and cut firewood for the kitchen stove year-round and for the heating stoves in the winter.

Usually on Mondays, boys and girls helped do the laundry outside. A big kettle full of water was heated over an open fire. To help, the children carried firewood and water and stirred the clothes. They cut slivers from bars of lye soap and dropped them in the kettle. Next, they wrung the water out of the clothes by hand and hung them on a line to dry. A few well-to-do farmers had washing machines. The agitator was moved by a lever, which a child could operate by moving back and forth. Most, however, had only washboards to scrub stubborn stains by hand.

Ironing also was a laborious task that children could do. Using solid-metal irons heated over a woodstove, ironing was hot, tiring work that required standing until the clothes were done.

In the spring, children helped with plowing the fields and the vegetable garden. In the summer, they helped with the hoeing and weeding. In the fall, they helped with the harvest. Fruits and vegetables had to be canned for the winter.

After the first frost, they helped with the slaughtering of hogs and salting pork and ham for the smokehouse. They ran water through wood ashes to make lye. Then hog lard was mixed with the lye to make soap.

In the winter, they cleaned chicken houses and barns and went into the woods to help bring in firewood. They did all this in addition to such routine chores as cooking, sewing, and cleaning house. Most farm families made their clothes, especially dresses for the females and shirts for the males. Little girls learned at an early age to sew by hand. The lucky ones learned to operate a treadle sewing machine that was pumped with the feet.

Whenever feed for the livestock or flour or meal was bought at the general store, women and girls often went along to pick out feed that was in sacks with good cloth and pretty patterns. As late as the 1930s and 1940s farm women and their daughters wore dresses that were called

Even small children could help feed farm animals. But then the animals had to be butchered for food. (State Historical Society of Missouri, Columbia)

"feed-sack dresses" by townspeople. Farm men and their sons wore feed-sack or flour-sack shirts.

In both the fall and the winter, boys and men hunted and trapped. Hunting for most farm families was not a sport; it was necessary if they were to have meat on the table. Furs and hides from hunting and trapping could be traded at the general store for goods. Or, in some instances, furs were traded for cash so the family could order shoes, firearms, traps, or tools from the Sears-Roebuck or Montgomery Ward catalogs. These catalogs were known as "wish books" to farm families because they knew they could only wish for many of the products in them.

Often children ran traplines on their walk to school in winter. Skunks, otters, mink, rabbits, and beavers were among the animals that farmers trapped to sell. Skunk fur was one of the most valuable furs and was judged by the fur buyer not only by its thickness but also by the width of the white stripe down its back. The wider the stripe, the better the fur. Ralph Rowden of Meta, Missouri, ran his traps every fall and winter morning on his walk to school. He said that often there was a strong odor of skunk among the children in the one-room school.

Such a labor-intensive life involved very little free time for children. Farmers depended on their sons and daughters for much of their labor. Because of this, farm families tended to be large by today's standards. It was not unusual for a farmer and his wife to have eight to twelve children living at home in a four- or five-room house. If the house became too crowded, some older farm boys slept in the barn.

When there were not enough children at home to do all the chores, a farmer had to barter with his neighbor for help. During the fall, for instance, neighboring farmers would gather to harvest one another's crops. Since many farmers used the barter system for farm supplies and labor, very few had cash to pay train fares of children from New York or to contribute to the society as Brace had hoped they would. But more hands to work were welcome.

Brace either knew little about children or chose to ignore the emotional wounds they would experience in their sudden removal from city life to the isolation and hard work of farm life. For most of the children, the trip was their first outside New York City.

They felt a full range of emotions, from delight, to awe, to fear. They saw rapidly changing scenery as the train moved along. For the first time, many of them saw orchards, fields of corn and wheat, and pastures with horses and cattle grazing.

As an "orphan train" crossed the country, it left part of its cargo at each stop, a few children in one small town and a few in another. Even though farmers needed many hands for labor, most of the small farm communities could not or would not take all of the children on the train. As the train moved to its next stop, those children not taken feared no one would ever want them.

Many children suffered great emotional stress at being uprooted from the city and shipped to a strange rural area. Most were separated from everyone they knew, including their brothers and sisters who may or may not have made the journey with them.

Robert Petersen felt all these emotions. "My first really vivid memory is sitting on a stage in the meeting hall in Blair, Nebraska, waiting for someone to take me, but no one did." Petersen eventually found a home, but some orphan-train riders were rejected in town after town. Sadly, they had to be returned to the New York City orphanages.

The greatest emotional wound resulted from separating children from the same family. Brace had not known, or chose to ignore, that the "bounty" of the Midwestern farmer was not so great that he could take a whole family of brothers and sisters. Separating children from the same family became routine as the orphan trains traveled west.

Despite the economic conditions of rural Midwestern life and the stress the children experienced, the orphan trains continued from their beginning in 1854 until 1929. During these years many thousands of children rode the trains west to a new life.

Brace's method of placing the children was simple. The Children's Aid Society sent notices to local postmasters announcing the time and date a trainload of orphans would arrive in each community. These notices would be posted in post offices, general stores, community centers, and churches. Ministers would announce from the pulpit the time and date of the arrival of the orphan train.

A meeting place to present the orphans was arranged by a local agent or committee. Small-town newspapers carried articles and advertisements describing the terms the society had developed for placing children with foster parents. On the train trip, a man and woman employed by the society as "western agents" took care of the children.

When the train arrived in a farm town, the agents took the children to the meeting place, such as a church, hotel,

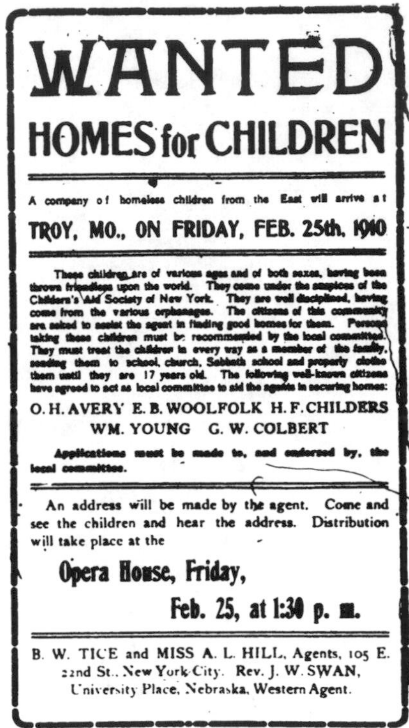

WANTED

HOMES for CHILDREN

A company of homeless children from the East will arrive at

TROY, MO., ON FRIDAY, FEB. 25th, 1910

These children are of various ages and of both sexes, having been thrown friendless upon the world. They come under the auspices of the Children's Aid Society of New York. They are well disciplined, having come from the various orphanages. The citizens of this community are asked to assist the agent in finding good homes for them. Persons taking these children must be recommended by the local committee. They must treat the children in every way as a member of the family, sending them to school, church, Sabbath school and properly clothe them until they are 17 years old. The following well-known citizens have agreed to act as local committee to aid the agents in securing homes:

O. H. AVERY E. B. WOOLFOLK H. F. CHILDERS
WM. YOUNG G. W. COLBERT

Applications must be made to, and endorsed by, the local committee.

An address will be made by the agent. Come and see the children and hear the address. Distribution will take place at the

Opera House, Friday,
Feb. 25, at 1:30 p. m.

B. W. TICE and MISS A. L. HILL, Agents, 105 E. 22nd St., New York City. Rev. J. W. SWAN, University Place, Nebraska, Western Agent.

Notices were posted in towns and published in local newspapers to let residents know when the orphan-train children would arrive. (State Historical Society of Missouri, Columbia)

or courthouse. Sometimes, when no other large gathering place was available, the agents presented the children at the train depot.

An unrecorded part of the selection process was that many agents rehearsed the children in ways they could attract attention so they would be selected quickly. Some children ran to one of the adults or to a couple and asked to be taken.

Stories about such events are found in the oral history and folklore of many towns on the orphan-train routes. Usually the children said something like, "Please, could I be your little boy?" Or, "I want to be your little girl."

People along the routes report that the children sang and danced to attract the attention of prospective parents. Many townspeople and farm families came to see the children simply out of curiosity. Some came looking for free

"A CARLOAD OF CHILDREN"

DISTRIBUTING HOMELESS LITTLE ONES SENT FROM THE EAST—SCENES IN A MISSOURI TOWN WHEN BOYS AND GIRLS SENT FROM NEW YORK BY THE CHILDREN'S AID SOCIETY CAME.

The village of Pilot Grove, Mo., saw last Friday an unusual and pathetic scene—the giving away of eighteen children from New York. The children were homeless little ones—orphans, foundlings, abandoned waifs—one three years old, some five, some seven, some nine, one as old as fifteen.

The children were sent out by the Children's Aid Society, an organization in New York that has existed some fifty years. Several shipments of children to the West to find homes among farmers has [*sic*] been made this summer, and about ninety children were placed this year in Missouri. The disposition of these eighteen children in Pilot Grove is typical of the disposition of the rest.

About a month ago B. W. Tice, agent for the Society, came to Pilot Grove and appointed a committee of five of the best known citizens of the town to help him to find homes for the children. These men were to decide on the merits of the persons who applied for children and to determine whether they were proper persons to rear and to care for them. The date of arrival had been advertised by handbills posted about in Cooper County. The children were to be taken to the Christian Church in Pilot Grove at 2:30 o'clock in the afternoon and there distributed. (*Kansas City Star,* October 21, 1900; reprinted in the Children's Aid Society's 1900 Annual Report)

labor. Others genuinely wanted to give a child a home. A committee of prominent local citizens, usually ministers and businessmen, screened the prospective foster parents who wanted to apply for a child.

An agreement was then signed between the western agent of the society and the foster parents. The agreement was printed on a card attached to the clothing of each child.

EMIGRATION DEPARTMENT
OF THE
CHILDREN'S AID SOCIETY OF NEW YORK.
CENTRAL OFFICE UNITED CHARITIES BUILDING.
105 East 22nd Street, New York City.

The Society reserves the right to remove a child at any time for just cause.

Date of placing ________________
Name of Child ________________
Age ________________
B. W. Tice, Agent

Willie Paul Dunnaway, who was on a train that went to Bentonville, Arkansas, reported that his foster parents chose him because he would not stay still on the stage. "I kept running around and tapping this bell that was on the table . . . pestering the others and ringing the bell. They said it showed ambition." When he got to his new home, his foster mother asked him what he wanted to drink for supper, milk or water. "I said 'I want beer,'" he recalled. "I must have had an interesting three and a half years in New York City." He considered himself the "most fortunate man on earth—that the people who adopted me and raised me were good." (Patrick-Sheets-Trickel Collection, Trenton, Mo.)

The back of the card served as a contract between the society and the foster parents.

> Terms on which the Children are Placed in Homes
>
> Applicants must be endorsed by the Local Committee.
>
> The child selected may then be taken to the home for mutual acquaintance, but no permanent arrangement will be considered until the home has been visited by the Placing-out Agent of the Society and the necessary papers signed.
>
> Children under 14 years of age, if not legally adopted, must be treated as members of the family, schooled according to the Educational Laws of the State, and comfortably clothed until they are 18 years old. It is then expected that suitable provision will be made for their future.
>
> Children between 14 and 16 years of age must be boarded and clothed until they are 18 when they are at liberty to make their own arrangements.
>
> Children over 16 years of age may be taken on a mutual agreement witnessed by the Agent of the Society or by a member of the local committee.
>
> Parties taking children agree to make reports of them to the Society twice a year, and to urge the children, if old enough, to write also. Removals of children proving unsatisfactory can be arranged through the local committee or an Agent of the Society, the party agreeing to retain the child a reasonable length of time after notifying the Society of the desired change.

The Children's Aid Society clearly wanted the child to become a part of the family and be provided for as a family member with food, clothing, and education. It gave children over sixteen more rights than younger children: older children could decide whether they would go with foster parents; younger ones could not.

Allowing for the removal of the child "proving unsatisfactory" gave the foster parents the right to decide to keep or return the child. But nothing in the agreement gave the child the opportunity to change his or her mind.

The agent of the society visited the child in his or her foster home once a year whenever possible. Largely, however, the society depended on letters from the foster parents and the children to guarantee the welfare of the orphans.

A BRIEF NARRATIVE.

BURLINGTON JUNCTION, MO., March 4th, 1882.

MR. MACY:—I am well. I have a sore arm. I fell out of the hay mow. We have a pet squirrel, it climbs up on my back, and comes in the house and gets some bread, and it climbs in your pocket and looks for hazel nuts. I read in the second reader. I feed the chickens; we have nine little chickens. I have a little ax. I can chop wood, and carry it in. I lead the horses to water. I drive hogs; I water hogs. I drive cattle; I water cattle. We have three little squirrels, they ain't got their eyes open.

WILLIE GUYETTE.

This procedure encouraged those who were happy and satisfied to write, while those who were not could be discouraged from writing by their foster parents. Also the parents could edit or not mail any letter they did not like. This loose supervision of the children, and of the adults who took them, led to much criticism of the society throughout the seventy-five years the orphan trains ran.

The criticism made of both the orphan trains of the Children's Aid Society and the Catholic Mercy Trains of the New York Foundling Hospital—that the children were used by their foster parents for cheap labor—has some basis in fact. Mina Hess reflected on her childhood memories in Minnesota:

> As a preschool child I remember that we had a family who went to the Twin Cities to get one of these orphans to help with the farm chores. The farmers had five small children so he (the orphan) had to help in the home also.

At age sixteen he was allowed to leave to seek his own fortune elsewhere. One day he came to our home to bid goodbye to my parents. We had just finished dinner. My mother fixed a good dinner spread for him. He ate as though he was real hungry, and talked to my parents about the abuse and beatings he had suffered; also that he had to eat scraps in the kitchen when the family was in the dining room.

He did not know where he was going to find a job but he was going to town to hitch a ride on a freight train. My mother packed a lunch for him and asked him to come to see us. Here his reply was "I'd like to come back and beat up that man who has mistreated me." This reply made an impression on my young mind as he seemed small and thin, blond and very nice looking. My parents and siblings prayed that God would take care of him. We never saw him nor heard from him.

THREE

The First Orphan Trains

Problems and Changes

In *The Dangerous Classes of New York,* Brace published long accounts of the early trains. Two of the western agents of the Children's Aid Society, E. P. Smith and C. R. Fry, also wrote about the first trains. Smith's report of the first trip, in 1854, to Dowagiac, Michigan, convinced the board of directors of the Children's Aid Society that future trains could relieve the pressure on the New York orphanages and provide good homes for the children.

The reports of Smith and Fry also provided the society with information that enabled them to plan the trips more carefully and to establish permanent policies for placement of the children with foster parents. As Brace wrote, "Since this first experience, we have always sent out children by regular trains, in decent style."

The society learned from the first trip west that the children should ride scheduled passenger trains, rather than boats or emigrant trains. Brace and Smith did not anticipate the problems with seasickness when forty-six boys and girls between the ages of ten and twelve were placed in steerage, below the top deck, on a riverboat from New York City to Albany, New York, and aboard a lake steamer from Buffalo to Detroit. The steerage section was cheap but crowded and uncomfortable.

Another problem Smith and the children faced on the trip was a six-hour wait for the emigrant train in Albany. Smith feared that the Albany street boys might lure his group of young orphans away. Some of the Albany boys did try this, but, instead, several of the orphan group convinced "John R.," an Albany street boy, to join them. The society, learning from this experience, established a policy against allowing children to join the group along the way because of the danger of legal problems.

Then Smith and the orphans faced overcrowding on the "emigrant train," which was really a freight train carrying passengers in boxcars. Smith wrote, "At the depot we worked our way through the Babel of at least one thousand German, Irish, Italians, and Norwegians."

The conductor had promised Smith that the orphans would be in a separate car, but the train station was crowded. The adult emigrants rushed aboard all the boxcars as soon as the doors were opened.

Once aboard, the orphans and Smith were intermingled with the emigrants. "There were scenes that afternoon and night which it would not do to reveal," Smith wrote. "Irishmen passed around bad whiskey and sang bawdy songs; Dutch men and women smoked and sang, and grunted and cursed; babies squalled and nursed, and left no baby duties undone." The lack of fresh air was made worse by the smoking of almost all of the male emigrants and many of the females.

The hardest part of the journey was at night. The boxcars were totally dark. Morning improved the situation greatly. The children were delighted to see the country scenery near Rochester, New York. Many of them had never seen farms or farm animals. Smith reported:

> Each one must see everything we passed, find its name, and make his own comments. "What's that, mister?" "A cornfield." "Oh, yes; them's what make buckwheaters." "Look at them cows (oxen plowing); my mother used to milk cows." As we whirled through orchards loaded with large, red apples, their enthusiasm

> rose to the highest pitch. It was difficult to keep them within doors.

Finally, the children reached Dowagiac, Michigan. By then their clothes were badly soiled and torn. Coal soot from the steam engines blew back into the cars and often covered the passengers with black dust, especially in the summer when the passenger-car windows were open. The children were completely worn out by the hard wooden benches of the boxcars.

The group was greeted by the congregation of the Presbyterian church of Dowagiac. But after the church service that

The city children on the orphan trains had heard many stories about the West, and they were full of questions. *Where to Emigrate and Why,* by Frederick B. Goddard, published in New York in 1869, was one of the many books of the time to promote moving west to start a new life "in some ideal spot among the broad fields and green pastures, the murmuring streams, and long valleys of the West or South," where "a happier home awaits." (State Historical Society of Missouri, Columbia)

Sunday, a problem arose. One of the orphans, a six-year-old boy, had wandered away and disappeared. However, by Monday evening the lost child was found, and the placement of the children continued. They were all in the homes of farm families by the following Saturday.

The application procedures had not been completely worked out yet. Each foster father and mother who wanted a child only had to present recommendations from a pastor and the justice of the peace. For later trains the society organized local committees to screen the foster parents before a child was placed with them. Smith gave no detailed accounting of the placement of the children on the first train; instead, he gave anecdotes.

"I have great hopes for the majority of them," he wrote. " 'Mag' is adopted by a wealthy Christian farmer. 'Smack' [John R., the boy who had voluntarily joined the train], the privateer from Albany, has a good home in a Quaker settlement. The two brothers, Dick and Jack, were taken by an excellent man and his son, living on adjacent farms. The German boy from the 'Lodging-house' lives with a physician in D—."

Smith also entertained his readers with anecdotes about city children who knew nothing about farm life. "Several of the boys came in to see me, and tell their experiences in learning to farm. One of them was sure he knew how to milk, and being furnished with a pail, was told to take his choice of cows in the yard. He sprang for a two-year old steer, caught him by the horns, and called for a 'line to make him fast.' "

The first trip involved many problems—traveling on the emigrant train, a temporarily lost child, and one boy who immediately ran away because he wanted to be placed with a farmer rather than a tinker (a man who mended pots and pans).

Despite the problems, Smith recommended that the society send more trains west. "On the whole, the first experiment of sending children west is a very happy one," he wrote, "and I am sure there are places enough with good families to give every poor boy and girl in New York a permanent home. The only difficulty is to bring the children to the homes."

Smith's optimism about good families in the West was enough to make the board of the Children's Aid Society establish western emigration as a major procedure in placing children under its care. Trains loaded with children started for the Midwest on a regular basis. By 1868, Children's Aid Society resident western agent Charles R. Fry could write even more optimistically than Smith about the successful placement of children in farm families.

In spite of Fry's enthusiastic report, the placement procedure in 1868 was still not as well developed as it later became. At first the society was transporting children in every age group. In Fry's January 1868 party, the ages ranged from one to twenty-one, and the twenty-one year old, Fry said, was "the greatest babe in the company."

This boy was a musician, and on the trip he played for the trainmen. Once they arrived in towns he went into saloons to play and encouraged other boys to join him in entertaining saloon customers for tips. Fry had to lecture the boys about going into saloons.

Within a day or two, the twenty-one year old had left the company, taking with him a concertina belonging to another boy. He had caused so much trouble among the younger children that Fry was relieved to find him gone. "The most of my trouble seemed to take wing and fly away with him. He was the scapegoat of the party."

Although there are later reports of the difficulty of placing children with handicaps, Fry, in his optimism, saw no problems with this among well-to-do, sympathetic farmers.

> One gentleman came in just for the purpose of seeing a little boy who had lost an eye, and was a brother to a boy his son had taken. When I told the little fellow that the gentleman lived near the man who had taken

> his brother, he climbed up on his knee, and putting his arms around his neck, said: "I want to go home with you and be your boy; I want to see my brother." The old gentleman wept, and wiping the tears from his eyes said: "This is more than I can stand; I will take this boy home with me."

Another instance of placing a handicapped child is found in the same report in the form of a letter from a deaf-mute Indiana farmer who had taken a deaf-mute child.

> C— H—, Ind., March 5, 1860.
>
> My Dear Sir—I received your kind letter some days ago. . . . First, . . . when you left D—, he cried and stamped on the floor by the door, but I took him to show him the horses; I told him when he will be a big man I would give him a horse. Then he quit crying, and began to learn A, B, C on that day when you left here. Now D— is doing very well, and plays the most of anything; he likes to stay here very well; he can learn about dog and cat. I am willing to take care of him [until he is] over twenty-one years old. Then I will give him a horse, money, clothes, school, etc. Last Saturday, D— rode on my colt himself; the colt is very gentle; on my advice, he got off the colt; he petted the colt most of time; he likes to play with the young colt. He likes to stay with me, and he said he doesn't want to go back where you are. He gathers chips and fetches wood for the stove, and is willing to do all his work directly. I wonder that he [is such a] bold boy and mocks some neighbors.
>
> Yours truly, friend,
> L. F. W.
>
> P. S. Write a letter to me immediately and let me know if I can keep him. He likes to go about with me, but not when it is very cold; I send him to stay in the house, out of the cold. When it is [a] warm day, he likes to go about with me. Sometimes he goes to town. He pets the colt every day; sometimes he waters the colt and feeds some corn himself.

Fry expressed the nineteenth-century faith in the rural ideal, which was the basis for the orphan trains, as he began placing the boys. "Illinois is a beautiful country. All the farmers seem to be wealthy. The larger boys, with two exceptions, were placed upon farms. Quite a number of boys came back to the hotel to say good-by, and thanked me for bringing them out."

These reports are so optimistic that it seems the society had no trouble placing children of any age or handicap with successful farmers. A more realistic view is apparent when we look at the language that Smith, Fry, and Brace used in their reports and at the way later policies of the society changed.

In the early reports the agents and Brace tend to refer to the adults with whom the children were placed as "employers." They often emphasized the wealth of the farmers receiving the children. Brace wrote, "Whenever practicable, the agent collects from the employers the railroad expenses, and otherwise obtains gifts from benevolent persons; so that frequently our collections and 'returned fares' in this way have amounted to $6,000 or $8,000 per annum."

Soon economic and social realities caused the board to adopt new policies that continued throughout the history of the trains. No very young children and no young adults, such as the twenty-one year old who had caused Fry so much trouble, were taken. The preferred ages of the children ranged between five and twelve. Both the society and the foster parents found that those between five and twelve could do some work on the farm and could become a part of the family.

Although the change in policy was not stated in writing, later reports show that the society did not continue to refer to the farmers and others who took children as employers. More emphasis was given to the concept of the foster parent and to "adoption."

In his reports Fry often referred to the wealth of the farmers of the Midwest and their ability to give to the society.

But, as Brace noted: "These gifts, however, are becoming less and less, and will probably eventually cease altogether; the farmer feeling that he had done enough in receiving the child." The truth was that most farm families were either unwilling or economically unable to take several children or to pay fifteen dollars to transport a child.

For practical reasons the society sometimes was forced to separate brothers and sisters. Brace was a kind man, but he was not sensitive to the significance of the biological family to the children. Henry Fawcett wrote in his book *Pauperism: Its Causes and Remedies* that street children were being treated better than the children of the working poor who attempted to take care of their children.

Brace wrote in answer to Fawcett, "We are perfectly ready to do the same for the outside, hard-working poor; but their

Jennie McDowell, the child in the white bonnet, came to Missouri on the orphan train in 1910. She was adopted by the Holman family, but the Holmans could not take her younger brother shown in the photo. He was moved around from home to home. (Annette Riley Fry Papers, 1882–1983, Western Historical Manuscript Collection–Columbia)

attachment to the city, their ignorance or bigotry, and their affection for their children, will always prevent them from use of such benefaction to any large degree." Brace saw the poor parents' "affection for their children" as a handicap that prevented their children from enjoying the ideal life that he imagined existed on Midwestern farms.

Although we now question some of the policies of the Children's Aid Society of New York, the motivation of Brace and the others was to help the homeless children. This is shown in his accounts of the various men and women, including Smith and Fry, who worked as "placing-out agents," "resident western agents," or in other capacities for the society. In praise of these workers, Brace wrote, "It is a matter of devout thankfulness that no accident has ever happened to any one of the many parties of children we have sent out, or to the agents."

Considering the methods of travel at that time, the numbers of children who traveled on the trains, and the fact that one agent was supervising twenty-five to thirty-five children on each trip, it seems miraculous that no accidents had occurred.

No doubt, Brace was only considering accidents involving broken bones or other major injuries. With thirty or so children riding the train, running about at each stop, and expressing curiosity at everything they saw, there must have been skinned knees and minor cuts and bruises of all kinds with plenty of tears to go around. Certainly the tasks of the agents were difficult.

In 1871, Brace wrote that E. Trott and J. P. Brace were "exceedingly able and judicious agents." Charles Loring Brace's daughter later wrote of her uncle, J. P. Brace: "His affection for the children made him a very kind caretaker during the long journey and his tact and pleasant manner everywhere won friends for the cause."

By 1871 the work of the agents enabled the efforts of the society to reach a new height at less expense than ever before. That year more than three thousand children were

Charles Loring Brace and others were convinced that sending children to rural areas gave them opportunities they would never have in New York. The trains continued to move thousands of children from the city to homes in the Midwest and West. (Kansas State Historical Society)

transported on the trains at an expense of $31,638, which included train tickets, food, and the agents' salaries.

Charles R. Fry aided Trott and J. P. Brace in arranging and supervising the placements. According to Charles Brace, Fry looked after "the interests of those previously sent" by making annual visits to the foster homes. He prepared the way for the next groups to be sent by arranging for local screening committees, sending out announcements about the arrival of the trains, and traveling from town to town explaining the work of the society.

John Macy, the assistant secretary of the society, was also directly involved with the placement and supervision of the orphans. His role was to carry on correspondence with

Children lined up to board an orphan train about 1920. (Patrick-Sheets-Trickel Collection, Trenton, Mo.)

thousands of people. He answered about two thousand letters a year, either from children who had been placed or from the adults with whom they had been placed.

From correspondence Macy received, the society was able to report that of the twenty-one thousand children sent on the orphan trains by 1871, only twelve had turned out to be criminals. And the number who ran away after being placed was too small to count. Macy also believed that the "system of sending families to the West was one of the best features of the Society."

However, even with a firm commitment to the system of transporting children to the Midwest, Macy still felt a need to defend the policy from criticism that names were changed and the religious backgrounds of the children were disregarded. He testified that the society had never changed the name of a child and that "Catholic children had often been entrusted to Catholic families."

His testimony hedges the question, however. The society did not prohibit the adults who took the children from changing not only their last names but their first names as well. It seems to have been a common practice for adults to change the name of the child they took, often without consulting the child.

In regard to religion, Brace apparently was so eager to place the children that his only requirement was that the home be Christian. So Catholic children were sometimes "entrusted" to non-Catholic families.

In fact, the children were entrusted to whatever family would take them and made members of whatever religious denomination the family had chosen for itself. Children were placed in a broad cross section of denominations, including minority groups such as Quakers. Catholic children were sometimes placed in Protestant homes. Jewish children were placed in Christian homes. For the society, religious differences were secondary to the ideal of a home with a rural family for the urban child.

Religious questions, along with questions about the welfare of the children, caused immediate and continuing criticism of the Children's Aid Society's western-emigration policy. These religious questions prompted the New York Foundling Hospital to start sending children on the Catholic version of orphan trains—the Mercy Trains, which began in 1869.

FOUR

Missouri

The Railroad Hub for Orphan Trains

Missouri was spanned from east to west by a railroad just before the Civil War. The construction crews, many of them Irish immigrants, finished laying the track from Hannibal to St. Joseph in 1859. Still, it was not until 1868 that the first bridge to take trains across the Mississippi River to Missouri was built at Quincy, Illinois. That rail line, known as the Quincy–St. Joseph Railroad, opened up more lands west of St. Louis for immigrants and settlers than ever before in U.S. history. Indeed, Missouri was now "the Mother of the West."

However, it was the accomplishment of James Eads, who bridged the Mississippi River at St. Louis in 1874, that enabled Missouri to become a hub for transportation to the West. Later in the century other bridges were built to span the Mississippi and bring trains to Missouri. The Rock Island bridge at Davenport, Iowa, brought trains to southern Iowa and northern Missouri. By late in the nineteenth century, trains crisscrossed the state, stopping to deliver and pick up passengers, freight, produce, grain, and livestock in almost every part of Missouri.

To encourage the building of railroads, the federal government had given companies rights-of-way in the West from ten to twenty-five miles wide, and sometimes as much as fifty. To raise money and encourage people to settle along the tracks and establish farms and ranches, the railroad companies then sold land along their rights-of-way.

New towns were established along the tracks by the railroad companies. There farmers and ranchers could ship their harvests and livestock back east and buy supplies. The first cattle drives from Texas ended in Sedalia on a trail that became known as "the Sedalia Trail." As the railroads pushed farther west, Kansas City and the Kansas towns of Abilene and Dodge became railroad centers for shipping cattle.

The flat farming country of northern Missouri became noted for its grain production. Railroad towns on the Rock Island line, such as Clarence, Ethel, and Elmer in northern Missouri, were named after the children of railroad-company executives. Other railroad towns were named for places in the East, such as Trenton, Missouri, on the Rock

The *Missouri* was piloted from Hannibal to St. Joseph in 1860 at an average speed of 50 miles per hour, covering 206 miles in a little more than four hours on April 8, 1860. The Civil War delayed expansion of the railroads, but after the war miles of railroad track were laid. In 1860, Missouri had 817 miles of track, according to historian Duane Meyer. By 1870 there were 2,000 miles of track, and by 1880 more than 4,000 miles. (State Historical Society of Missouri, Columbia)

Island line, named for Trenton, New Jersey, and Newburg, Missouri, on the Frisco line, named for Newburgh, New York.

The terms *whistle-stop, tank town,* and *roundhouse* became a part of the language. The orphan-train riders became familiar with these words as they rode west into Missouri. A whistle-stop was a small town where trains stopped only when signaled by the station agent or a ticket buyer.

Later the term *whistle-stop* referred to any town where trains stopped only long enough for the engineer to blow the whistle of the locomotive. Still later, the term referred to short stops at railroad stations in a political campaign.

President Harry Truman conducted what is probably the most famous whistle-stop political campaign in history to defeat Thomas Dewey in 1948. Most of the political polls showed he had no chance to win. But along the whistle-stops, Truman drew such large crowds that one of his advisers, Clark Clifford of St. Louis, realized in October that Truman was going to win the November election.

President Truman, who grew up in a whistle-stop town called Lamar in Barton County, had begun his political career as a county judge in rural Jackson County, Missouri. He shared with Brace a belief in the rural ideal and an awareness that the people of the whistle-stop communities understood plain speaking and honest efforts to solve social problems.

Tank towns were similar in size to whistle-stop towns. These special towns along the railroad tracks had water towers or ponds where the steam engines could fill their water tanks. In Rolla, Missouri, the Frisco Pond is now a recreational area. Once it provided water for steam engines. The orphan-train riders soon learned that the engineer had to stop every fifty to one hundred miles "to take on water." The frequency of stops for water depended on the length of the train and the steepness of the grades on the line.

Another railroad term that the orphans riding the trains learned was *roundhouse.* These were buildings where steam engines could be turned around on a turntable. Kenneth Roach, who was a station agent on the Frisco Railroad for many years, said Newburg was chosen as a location for switching engines because it was in a natural geological depression in the Little Piney River valley. The switchyard engine could easily push the train engine to start it coasting down into the roundhouse. There the engine could be turned. An engine that was pointed west could then go east.

Roundhouse became a common word in the U.S. vocabulary. Prize fighters lost fights when they led with a roundhouse right. Baseball players found the roundhouse curveball impossible to hit. One hot Sunday in July in 1951, Tom Henley of Eugene, a whistle-stop on the Missouri-Pacific line, won both games of a doubleheader throwing almost nothing but roundhouse curveballs.

The word *doubleheader* is also a baseball term that came from the railroads. Trains had to add a second steam engine to climb steep grades. The two engines formed a doubleheader.

Georgia Greenleaf, one of the Children's Aid Society's western agents, had to wait on a sidetrack near the roundhouse in Newburg with her trainload of orphans for a second engine to be connected to their train before they went on to Lebanon. This doubleheader of engines could climb the grade at the Dixon Cut, named because the construction crews had cut through an Ozark mountain to make the grade less steep.

The long grade up to the town of Dixon must have seemed unending for the orphans. Even with a second engine, the train could only go about five to ten miles an hour. The orphans must have had fear and doubts about their future as the train moved slowly along toward Lebanon where they would be offered as foster children to the adults waiting at the train station.

How would their foster parents feel about them? How would the people in town treat them? Would they make new friends among the children at school? Would they ever see their biological family again?

The St. Louis and San Francisco Railroad Company (known as the Frisco) was such a part of the lives of the people of Newburg, Dixon, Richland, and the other whistle-stop or tank towns along the line that they named their public-school athletic conference the Frisco League. The league still exists, even though the Frisco line became first a part of the Burlington-Northern Railroad and is now part of the Santa Fe Railroad.

The whistle-stops, tank towns, and towns with roundhouses, including the towns of the Frisco League, were ideal destinations for the riders of the orphan trains. To fill up their new towns and to sell farmland, the railroads offered cheap fares to people moving west. Charles Loring Brace recognized that the growth of the railroads in Missouri and throughout the nation was what he needed for his plan to work.

He was using the new technology of the nineteenth century to solve a difficult social problem. Today orphan homes and social workers use the technology of videos, computers, and the Internet to make a connection between homeless children and prospective parents. Perhaps this modern technology is less stressful and dangerous for children. Nevertheless, Brace effectively used the nineteenth-century technology of railroads in his orphan-train plan.

For fifteen dollars he could buy a ticket to send an orphan from New York City to a new home in Missouri. Cheap fares, the central location of the state, and numerous small farming towns along the railroad tracks made Missouri a hub for the orphan trains even though many areas of the state were still considered to be "the Wild West."

When the trains first started bringing orphans to Missouri, Jesse and Frank James and their cousins, the Younger brothers, were still robbing trains and banks. Farther west in Kansas, the Daltons were making their names as outlaws. Probably some of the more adventurous orphans were hoping to see a train robbery or meet an outlaw. Others probably hoped they would not see any outlaws.

Most of the children probably had a very colorful view of the West from reading the dime novels about such western heroes as Deadeye Dick, Wild Bill Hickok, or Buffalo Bill. Some may have read about Hickok's shoot-out in Springfield that became the model for many accounts of western gunfights in books. Others may have seen or read about Buffalo Bill's Wild West show when it was in New York. It was an exciting but unrealistic version of the West, with the Congress of Rough Riders and Sitting Bull and other Sioux and Cheyennes who had killed General George Custer and his troops at the battle of Little Big Horn.

Certainly the children expected to see cowboys and Indians when they crossed the Mississippi River. However, by the time the railroads were built, most Missouri Indians had moved to Oklahoma. But cowboys were very much a part of the state. Many of the boys who rode the trains must have thought they too could become cowboys instead of farm boys. Their dreams were not far-fetched. Cattle ranching was as labor-intensive as farming, and the cowboys of the ranches often were between fourteen and eighteen years old.

Even if they could not become cowboys, they dreamed they would have horses to ride on the farms of their foster parents. But most Missouri farmers used mules or oxen. By that time, the Missouri mule had become famous for its strength, stamina, and agility as a farm animal. Farmers throughout the United States wanted Missouri mules. The mules were so surefooted they could cultivate rows of crops without crushing the plants.

The horses that farmers did have were big-boned draft or work horses, not suitable for riding. Few quarter horses or cow ponies were found on Missouri farms then. These small animals did not have the strength or stamina for working from daylight to dark in hot Missouri summers.

Billy Frank had dreams of having his own horse after he was placed with a farm family near Trenton, Missouri. His

Billy Frank was eleven when he came to Trenton, Missouri, on one of the last orphan trains. He was taken home by Fred and Sadie Dickman, and his foster mother reported he loved horses and sometimes got to ride them. In World War II he received a battlefield commission in New Guinea. (Patrick-Sheets-Trickel Collection, Trenton, Mo.)

foster family did not have horses. So when her husband went to town, his foster mother let Billy ride the milk cow. Even though this was not good for the production of milk, his new mother wanted Billy to be happy.

The dreams of the girls on the train may have involved less adventure than the dreams of the boys. The girls might have hoped to marry a farmer or rancher and have a home and family. Or they thought of becoming schoolteachers in the one-room schoolhouses they passed as the train moved farther and farther west. But they doubtless had heard of the Missouri outlaw Belle Starr and the Missouri adventuress Calamity Jane from folktales or from reading dime novels. So some girls may well have had dreams of possible adventure. However, the immediate future of the boys and girls who rode the orphan trains to Missouri depended on the adults who took them at the next stop.

Many citizens of the whistle-stop communities and tank towns had been prepared to accept the orphans out of kindness. The sentimental folk songs of the day such as "The Orphan" and "The Orphan Girl" had created sympathy for homeless children.

In 1906, Henry Belden of the University of Missouri organized the members of the Missouri Folklore Society to collect folk songs popular in the state in the early twentieth century, just as the orphan trains were making their most frequent trips to the state.

"The Orphan Girl," collected in 1906 from C. H. Williams of Bollinger County, focuses on the cruelty of a rich man not willing to give a home to a child.

> 'Twas cold and dark and the snow fell fast,
> But the rich man shut his door,
> And his proud lips curled as he rudely said,
> "No home, no bread for the poor."

"The Orphan" was collected by the Missouri Folklore Society from Sarah Henry of Saline County in 1913, but she had known the song since about 1870. It is sad enough to make even the most hard-hearted adult want to take a child from an orphan train.

> Will you hear my mournful story?
> All my friends are dead and gone,
> Father is no more, nor mother;
> I'm an orphan left alone.

The children rode trains into the state on now almost-forgotten lines—the St. Louis and San Francisco (the Frisco); the Rock Island; the Missouri-Pacific (MoPac); the Wabash; and the Missouri, Kansas, and Texas (the Katy). To get to the whistle-stops and tank towns, they often had to leave

Many agencies and organizations tried to find homes for orphans. (State Historical Society of Missouri, Columbia)

the main lines and take branches or spur lines on passenger trains that local residents called "puddle jumpers" and "milk trains." These trains traveled very slowly because they stopped at every station and sometimes at crossroads and farms to pick up milk and passengers.

Trains had become such a part of life in the United States that Brace used railroad terms for the titles he gave the adults who accompanied the children on the trains. Just as the railroads had station agents, freight agents, ticket agents, and passenger agents, the Children's Aid Society had western agents or placing-out agents. The society's agents continued to be the keys to the success of the orphan trains.

The men and women serving as western agents cared for the children on the trains, arranged for their placement, and made annual visits to foster homes. The society used many different agents in the placement process over the seventy-five-year history of the orphan trains. The Reverend and Mrs. J. W. Swan and Georgia Greenleaf were among the most active of the agents for the society.

The Reverend Mr. Swan, who was born in Illinois in 1851, moved to Nebraska with his parents at the age of four. He entered the Methodist ministry in his early adulthood and served churches in Nebraska until 1905. While active as a minister in 1903, he served as a local contact between the Children's Aid Society and the towns where the orphans were placed.

Because of his success in this role, the society offered him a full-time job as a western agent in 1904. Missouri's central location caused him to establish his permanent home in Sedalia on the Missouri-Pacific line. In his new job he traveled to and from New York to bring groups of children coming west. He rode trains to small Midwestern towns to supervise the placement of the children. He visited foster homes to make follow-up reports on the children each year. He wrote reports for the society and letters to foster parents.

Swan's second wife, Hattie, also served as an agent for the society. Both seemed to have ideal temperaments for their jobs. Many children remembered the Swans for their gentleness and sense of humor.

Once as they were getting off a train with about twenty children in Sedalia, a passerby asked the Reverend Mr. Swan, "Are all these children yours?" Swan answered, "Yes, every one of them." To the children he was always "Grandpa Swan" even after they had found new homes. Many wrote him letters throughout their lives—addressed to "Grandpa Swan."

Noah Lawyer of St. Joseph, in recalling his trip with his three brothers on an orphan train, said that he remembered Swan as a short, round man with a ready smile who was always nice and kind.

Others recall that he made sure to visit the children after they were placed. On some occasions, children were found to be unsuited to their new family. Swan and his wife took these children into their own home until permanent homes could be found for them.

A letter from their daughter, Dorothea Swan Menke, described one of the last orphan trains her parents brought to Missouri:

> The year was 1927 and I was delegated to make the trip to New York with my parents to bring a company of children to Palmyra, Missouri, for placement. (This was my graduation gift.) We took the trip on the Missouri Pacific Rail Road as it ran out of Sedalia and my parents were given passes on this line as well as the M K & T . . . called Katy RR.
>
> It was shortly after we arrived in New York and were on the bus when there were a lot of horn honking and then we saw a plane and we learned this was Charles Lindberg [*sic*] when he made his non-stop transatlantic flight. There were small pieces of paper (resembling bills) flying everywhere and people picking them up. It was an exciting thing to see.
>
> I cannot remember much about the Orphanage Building. It did not seem large to me. The smaller children were all sleeping in individual beds in one room. I cannot remember any tour of the Orphanage. Everything looked nice and clean.
>
> In our company there were ten or eleven children, ranging in ages of 3 to 12 or so. The children looked nice and I am sure they were pleased to know they were taking a long train ride. They were well behaved and seemed to enjoy themselves on the train trip. We ate some hot meals and a few snacks. It seems to me we slept in the chairs but am not sure. If the train stop was long enough for us to go outside we tried to walk together. My father had a lot of dry wit and to see that many children people would ask him if they were all his. He replied yes, they are in my care. Then he would smile and tell his story.
>
> When we arrived at Palmyra we went directly to the Theatre. Everything seemed to move smoothly. I think the homes had been visited and chosen if children suited the people who were to take them. Some visited

> with the children before their mind was made up but all the children in that company were placed. If the new parents could take 2 of a family it was good and then if more in that family they would try to place the rest in that Community so the children could keep in touch. Visits were made shortly after placement to see if all was going well and if a child must be removed for some reason (usually they came to our house to stay until a new place was found for them). I think a number of visits were made the first year to see that all was going well. My parents said they wanted the children placed where they were loved and were one of the family. Follow-up visits were important also. As I recall most of the company did continue in these homes. Years after placement I remember during my early years some of the children would come by and this was always a joy to my parents.
>
> P.S. I should mention when we went to the Recreation Hall or Theatre in Palmyra, . . . the children went in a group on the stage and the names were called so the new parents would know their child. It went smoothly and certainly did not take long.

A news story of April 17, 1929, from the *Trenton Republican-Times* shows how highly esteemed the Reverend Mr. Swan was in the towns along the orphan-train stops.

> The nine boys brought here for adoption by Mr. and Mrs. [J. W.] Swan, the former of whom is the Missouri agent for the Children's Aid Society of New York, have all been placed in homes, and Mr. and Mrs. Swan will leave for their home at Sedalia, Missouri, tomorrow, it was learned today. . . .
>
> Few here will dispute the children, as placed are all in fine homes and Mr. and Mrs. Swan have done all in their power to see all of the children have been well located.

When the Reverend Mr. Swan died in 1934, his work with the orphan trains was featured in his obituaries. Newspapers and residents of Missouri recalled his work with the children as his finest achievement. He and his wife are remembered in Sedalia as people of great kindness and generosity.

One of the stories repeated among Sedalia residents is about one little girl, Elsie, who could not be placed in a foster home because her face was disfigured. The Swans adopted her as their daughter. Sedalia residents also remember that the Swans would have as many as seventeen children living with them at one time.

Less is known about Georgia Greenleaf. She had relatives and friends in Lebanon, Missouri, on the Frisco line, and she was often able to find temporary homes there for children who had not been taken at other train stops. Then they would not have to be returned to New York immediately. Those who came on the trains remember her as a dignified woman of great kindness and devotion to the children. She

Georgia Greenleaf was praised by the children she cared for on the orphan trains. One reported that she really listened to them and faithfully visited them in their foster homes. (Patrick-Sheets-Trickel Collection, Trenton, Mo.)

took her role as western agent for the society as a life's calling and never married.

Even less is known of other western agents of the society. They apparently were devoted to their work and held themselves to high standards of conduct. The society has no documents criticizing them. Orphan-train riders who are still living are unanimous in their praise of the agents.

Despite the continued positive reports of the society and the work of such western agents as the Reverend Mr. and Mrs. Swan and Georgia Greenleaf, criticism of the trains continued. The society continued to try to find ways to measure its work. Brace noted that in the 1870s the New York City Police Department reports showed fewer arrests of children for homelessness, thievery, petty larceny, and juvenile delinquency. Also, fewer were imprisoned as pickpockets and purse snatchers. Brace concluded that the reduction in the crime rate among children when the population of New York City was growing rapidly was a direct result of the orphan trains.

In 1898, Brace's son Robert surveyed the children from fifteen groups placed in northern Missouri, Iowa, eastern Nebraska, and Kansas. He concluded that 90 percent were doing well.

In its report for 1900 the society stated that the records of all the younger children placed in foster homes up to that time showed that 87 percent were doing well. But these statistics are somewhat misleading. The groups surveyed did not include teenagers who had been "placed in situations at wages." The society found older children harder to keep track of than smaller children.

The society's transportation of children was at its height around the turn of the century. It was sending out more than three thousand children each year to the Midwest and South. In 1917 the society listed in its annual report the successful people who had ridden the trains as another measure of its effectiveness.

> A Governor of a State, a Governor of a Territory, two members of Congress, two District Attorneys, two Sheriffs, two Mayors, a Justice of the Supreme Court, four Judges, two college professors, a cashier of an insurance company, twenty-four clergymen, seven high school Principals, two School Superintendents, an Auditor-General of the State, nine members of State Legislatures, two artists, a Senate Clerk, six railroad officials, eighteen journalists, thirty-four bankers, nineteen physicians, thirty-five lawyers, twelve postmasters, three contractors, ninety-seven teachers, four civil engineers, and any number of business and professional men, clerks, mechanics, farmers, and their wives, and others who have acquired property and filled positions of honor and trust. Nor would the roll call be complete without mention of four army officers and 7,000 soldiers and sailors in their country's service.

Partially in reaction to the criticism that the society was converting Catholic children to Protestantism by its system of placing children, the Catholic Charities of New York had also started sending trains of orphans west on what the nuns called "Mercy Trains." The Catholic trains were managed by the New York Foundling Hospital, which had been established in 1869 by the Sisters of Charity of St. Vincent de Paul.

Since its beginning, the New York Foundling Hospital had taken in babies that had been left in gutters, in barrels, on doorsteps, or wherever else a parent could leave them. The nuns of St. Vincent even placed a cradle in the main hall of the hospital so that mothers could anonymously leave their newly born babies.

Soon the hospital had more babies than cradles and beds. It began to place children through the parish priests of the Midwest and South. The Children's Aid Society had depended on finding foster parents and homes for the children after the trains arrived in each town. That meant the children had to wait and wonder if they would be chosen.

Sister Irene of the New York Foundling Asylum, established by the Sisters of Charity of St. Vincent de Paul in 1869, put a crib in the entry to the home so that a new mother could safely leave a baby she could not care for. "Here no questions were asked, no demands were made, but help and comfort were always waiting." (Shirley Andrews Collection)

The Catholic trains took only those children who had been placed before the train left from New York City. This policy assured the child that he or she was wanted before being taken from the orphanage. For each child, the sisters of the hospital made a new suit or dress with his or her name and the name of the new parents pinned on the inside of the back collar.

Irma Craig Schnieders was one of the orphans who came to Osage City in Cole County, Missouri, on the Mercy Trains. She had kept a record of other children who came on the train with her and later wrote an account of her arrival in Missouri.

> I was born in New York according to my birth records from St. Vincent's Foundling Hospital, on the 5th day

> of July, 1898. My father's name was Walter Craig and my mother's name was Lida Steinberg Craig. My father was a draftsman and was 43 years old and my mother was 30 years old at the time of my birth. I was brought to the Foundling Home when I was 58 days old by my mother, and I was baptized on Sept. 6, 1898. I haven't been able to get any records of my parents' whereabouts after that.
>
> The orphans were "indentured," meaning that a couple signed an agreement, not legal, that they would treat the child well. I was placed with a couple named George and Katherine Boehm on May 19, 1901.

Years later Sister Evelyn, Mrs. Schnieders's daughter, had an interview with Sister Augustine at the Foundling Hospital located in St. Vincent Ferrer parish, "in a very elite district":

> and she told Sr. Evelyn how a sister would take between 20 and 40 little ones on the train in response to several Pastors finding good homes for the children. How it was a struggle to get fresh milk for a long trip, especially when spending the night at a railroad siding. Sometimes the sisters would make the social service calls themselves, sometimes it was done by hired local people, and often by the parish priest.
>
> I was about 33 months old, when with 35 others, I arrived at the Osage City railroad station. Mrs. Boehm would tell how I had accepted her and had said: "This is my mama." I'm sure the sisters had prepared us for this meeting before.

Unfortunately, Mrs. Boehm died when Irma was ten years old. Because she missed her foster mother so much, her foster father decided she should live with the Rackers family. Adeline Rackers Gnagi and her brother, John Rackers, agreed to take Irma and make her a part of their family.

Irma Schnieders wrote about her new home: "This home was even better than the first one. They had a large rambling house where I could play upstairs to my heart's content."

Irma Craig arrived in Osage City, Missouri, on May 19, 1901, on a Mercy Train or "Baby Train" sent west by the New York Foundling Hospital. She had been asked for by George and Katherine Boehm of Taos in Cole County. A neighbor gave her the broom as a present. (Shirley Andrews Collection)

She did have a problem with language at first. Her native tongue was English. Her first foster family spoke High German, and the second spoke Low German. But Irma adjusted to these language differences, and as an adult she was still able to speak some High German, which she had learned in school.

She also vividly remembered the other children on the train in her autobiography.

> Some of the children were barely 18 months old, and some were 4 and 5 years old. Cecelia Titus was almost four, [and] recalls how she resisted going to her new parents, Mr. and Mrs. Henry Sommers from Osage Bend, and had said: "That's not my mama." When

After her foster mother died when she was ten, Irma Craig went to live with the Rackers family, where she had an older foster sister, Mary, and lots of room to play. (Shirley Andrews Collection)

> they stopped at Plassmeyer's Store at Wardsville, Mr. Plassmeyer asked them if that was their new little girl, Cecelia piped up and quickly said, "But I'm not going to stay with them." When they were ready to go home they found Cecelia upstairs, she says that she remembers looking for Charley, her playmate at the orphan home. I didn't remember that day very long, but I always did know that I was an orphan.

Irma Schnieders has listed in her autobiography other orphans from her group who came to Osage City and grew up in nearby communities in Osage and Cole Counties.

Some were taken to Jefferson City, but not all kept their own names. One of the children, Magdalene Donner, was raised in Taos by Father Joseph Schmidt and his housekeeper, Helena Sutterer. She remembers that Magdalene had beautiful dark-red hair and was fun to play with.

Irma Schnieders felt that she and other children were fortunate to have come to Missouri on orphan trains, or

Father Joseph Schmidt of St. Francis Xavier Church in Taos, Missouri, helped find homes for children sent to central Missouri by the New York Foundling Hospital. He was a native of Ramsdorf, Westphalia. Irma Craig sometimes stayed in the rectory when the weather was too bad to get home, and she remembered that his housekeeper baked wonderful pumpernickel bread. (courtesy Parish Family, St. Francis Xavier Church, Taos, Mo.)

the Mercy Trains, but many native Missourians wanted the trains stopped.

Perhaps because of accusations that it was converting Catholic children to Protestantism or perhaps because of its white Anglo-Saxon leadership, the Children's Aid Society of New York did not openly concern itself with Jewish, Asian, black, or Catholic children. Brace was sometimes a practical man; he probably recognized that placing these children in the rural Midwest or the South, among mostly Anglo-Saxon Protestant families, would be difficult, if not impossible.

He was very likely also sensitive to the fact that placement of black children could lead to accusations that the society was engaging in involuntary servitude. Nevertheless, in the lore and history of many Midwestern families, there are stories of children from racial, ethnic, and religious minorities coming on the trains.

Mary Hamilton Bracken Phillips of Blackwater in Saline County heard from her father about a Jewish boy who grew

Irma Craig graduated from the eighth grade in 1913. After obtaining a teacher's certificate, she taught in Schnieders Bridge School. In 1922 she and Robert Schnieders were married. They settled on a farm west of Jefferson City, where their eight children were born. After her husband died in 1939, she continued to live in their home until her own death in 1989. Mrs. Schnieders felt that the Mercy Trains enabled many children to have better lives. (Shirley Andrews Collection)

up in his home. "When I asked him where he came from, father said he didn't know." The boy, about twelve years old, just got off the train and walked up the hill, and his mother brought the boy home. "I asked what his name was; Father said he took the name Bracken."

The Bracken family lore is vague about the boy. Mary Phillips's brother, who died in 1984, said that he thought the boy's first name was Sam and that he later continued to live in Blackwater. Mrs. Phillips is still searching for further information about him.

Elizabeth Senger Mann has written about her family's experience with a child of another race from the orphan trains.

> My aunt, Rachel Marie Donnivan Saenger was one of the orphans. She was adopted by my grandparents in Pierce City, Lawrence County, Missouri. She was born in New York about 1892. She died at the age of 67. I am interested in finding out more about her family. . . . They never mentioned it. I was a teenager before I knew she was adopted. She was always one of the family. She had some negro blood but that was never mentioned. I only learned this from my friend's mother when I was in High School.

Stories about child abuse and marriages between orphans of unknown parentage or race and locally born residents caused the state legislature to pass a bill in 1901 forbidding orphan trains. The law mentions the Children's Aid Society by name.

The bill was introduced by Sen. John Clay of St. Francois County, a rural area of small farms and whistle-stops that is an almost perfect model for Brace's plan. The language of the law reveals a great deal about people's attitudes. Section 3 of the law reads: "The necessity for this act going into effect at once [is] on account of the fact that the New York children's aid society is pouring car loads of children into the state without properly supervising them."

The law passed with penalties ranging from jail terms of thirty days to fines of from five to one hundred dollars. Apparently, the law was never enforced. The orphan trains and the Catholic Mercy Trains kept coming to Missouri for twenty-eight more years.

One of the last orphan trains of the Children's Aid Society came to Missouri in 1929. By then, most states had passed stricter adoption laws and policies. Many eastern states and cities assumed more responsibilities in caring for orphans, and so the trains were no longer needed.

FIVE

New Missourians Separated from Their Families

The emotional pain from not knowing his or her biological family runs through every orphan's story. Perhaps an even greater feeling of loss came from knowing that somewhere there were family members he or she would never see again.

Many Missouri orphan-train riders suffered such losses. At times the Children's Aid Society was careless in separating children from their living parents. Such was the case of Jimmie Doyle, or "Zimmie" as he was known to his mother. He came to Princeton, Missouri, on an orphan train in the first decade of the twentieth century.

In a letter, Jimmie Doyle's mother tells of her love for "Zimmie" and his sister, Dora. For economic reasons and educational opportunities, Rachel Doyle had sent Jimmie and Dora to a new Lutheran boarding school in New York City. Jimmie had cried and had not wanted to leave his mother. Rachel had promised she would visit them as often as she could. But times were hard for her.

Rachel Doyle had lived with the children's father in poverty for fourteen years. Often she had nothing to feed the children but potatoes and gravy. Once she stole a ten-pound sack of flour to keep them from starving.

The living conditions became so unbearable that she left her husband to take a job as a cleaning woman in a hotel in Cobblesville, New York. There she made $2.50 a week, spending $2 a week for someone to take care of her children. Then she became ill and was not able to work.

For the next three months, a kind black woman living nearby cared for Rachel Doyle and her two children. When Rachel recovered, she took a job as a housekeeper for a priest. Then a man offered to give her and the two children a home. Rachel and the man were not "legally married," she wrote, "only sworn together." Shortly after she moved into a new home, Rachel let Jimmie and Dora go to the boarding school in New York City. She never saw them again.

For unknown reasons, they were sent to Missouri on an orphan train. There they were placed in separate foster families. Almost immediately after taking Jimmie, his foster family, the Powells of Princeton, Missouri, wrote a letter of inquiry to the Children's Aid Society asking about his biological parents.

Jimmie's mother wrote the Powells, explaining how "this horrible thing happened." She explained that at the Sunday school the children attended, some of the women had persuaded Dora to go to the boarding school in the city. Dora wanted to go, and Jimmie's mother agreed to send both children. She had seen them off at the local train station with no idea she would never see them again. Until she had heard from the Powells, she did not know what had happened to either child.

She went on to write that although she was "lonely and sorrowful," she did not have the money to come to Missouri to get her son. She had decided he was better off with the Powells. Jimmie Doyle remained with his foster parents until he reached adulthood.

The pain of the separation from his mother and his sister was apparently so great that he never mentioned it to his children. His daughter, Mary Turek, said he "never told us anything." It was only after his death that his biological mother's letter was found in his effects.

Not only the poor suffered the pain of separation. Deborah and Kathleen Scott were separated from their mother when they came to Gallatin, Missouri, on June 26, 1905. Kathleen Scott's daughter, Betty Moore, has saved many of the mementoes from her mother's orphan-train experience, including the card pinned to her dress and the newspaper article that described their placement. The card gives the child's name, age, and the date of placement. The newspaper article describes the procedure the Children's Aid Society followed in placing the children.

> FOUND HOMES
> Good homes were found for the ten children brought here from New York by Rev. J. W. Swan last Thursday. There were so many applications for the children that the trouble of the local committee was mostly confined to making selections that would be to the best interests of the children and their foster parents. The meeting was advertised for the Y.M.C.A. rooms and they proved entirely too small and a change was made to the Cumberland Presbyterian Church, the use of which was generously proffered by Rev. H. F. Smith. Every seat in the large church was occupied. It was indeed an affecting scene as the little ones were divided out, though so far as possible those of the same family were sent into the same neighborhood. There were two bright little sisters, and fortunately an application for both of them was made by M. A. Scott, a wealthy farmer living near Lock Springs in Livingston County and the committee was unanimous in placing them with him.

The day the train arrived in Gallatin, Mrs. Scott had gone to the station prepared to take one girl. When she saw the two "bright little sisters" clinging to each other, she could not bear to see them separated. She told her family, "I had to take them both."

The Scotts then began the process of legally adopting the sisters. Soon the lawyer they hired to prepare the adoption papers made a startling discovery. The two sisters, Deborah and Kathleen, had come from a wealthy New York family named Reed, and their mother was still living. Their mother immediately contacted the Scotts and gave them an explanation of how she and her daughters had been separated.

She and her husband had left the two under the care of a governess in New York City while they traveled in Europe. They had sent money to the governess for the care of the children. After a time, the governess had lost touch with the parents. Not knowing what else to do, she had turned the two girls over to the Children's Aid Society. They had been placed in an orphanage for a time and then sent to Missouri on an orphan train.

By the time their mother had come back from Europe, she was separated from her husband. After realizing that her daughters had disappeared, she had hired a detective who located them in Missouri.

Legally, the Scotts had to return the sisters to their biological mother. In spite of their emotional attachment to the girls, and the tears of the girls when they were told that they would have to go back to New York, the Scotts prepared to send them back.

Then their mother decided they would be better off with the Scotts. So the children stayed in Missouri and grew up in the Scott family. But they were never legally adopted. The lawyer for the Scotts advised against adoption because the sisters might lose their inheritance from their biological parents.

Throughout their childhood, their mother kept in contact and sent gifts from her travels. When she was dying, she asked that her daughters be sent to her. That was the only time she had asked to see them. Kathleen went back to New York to see her, but Deborah did not. Both sisters continued to live in Missouri for the rest of their lives.

Putting children on an orphan train without the knowledge of the parents was not a common practice of the Children's Aid Society. But separation of children in the same family was. Too often it was just as the article in the Gallatin newspaper quoted above reported it was: "It was indeed an affecting scene as the little ones were divided out, though so far as possible those of the same family were sent into the same neighborhood."

One can imagine it was an "affecting scene" as children from the same family cried over being separated from one another. The journalist who wrote the article probably did not think about the appropriateness of his phrase "little ones were divided out," but divided they were.

Frank and Rose Cranor, brother and sister, were separated early in their journey on an orphan train to Missouri. Rose broke her leg on the train and had to be hospitalized. Frank continued on the trip and found a foster home in Albany, Missouri, in February 1917, with the Swetnam family.

Rose Cranor fell and broke her leg on the trip west, and her brother Frank was sent ahead with other children to Albany in Gentry County, Missouri. When she arrived in Albany in March 1917 her foster mother had arranged for her brother to be there. The children were delighted to see one another, even though they knew they would be living in separate homes. (Patrick-Sheets-Trickel Collection, Trenton, Mo.)

Rose, fully recovered, arrived in Albany in March and was placed with Mr. and Mrs. William Whitton. Although they grew up in different families, Frank and Rose were able to see each other almost every day. In recalling her journey on the orphan train, Rose said:

> I was brought to what used to be the Merchants Hotel. I remember being at the hotel. There were fourteen other children with my brother who came a month earlier, but I was alone when I came. Mr. Swan of the Children's Aid Society came once a year after that to interview us to see if we were well taken care of and happy in our new homes.

Thirteen years later, in 1930, Frank returned to New York and, with the help of the Children's Aid Society, tried to find information about his biological parents. He was able to locate his father in 1942. His father told Frank that his mother had left the family when Rose was only two weeks old.

For a time their father had tried to care for them. He had had to leave them with the landlady of the tenement where they lived when he went to work. Soon he had realized he would have to give them up.

Rose remembered her father:

> He was very good to us. He was a chauffeur, wore a uniform, and he was friends with Charlie Chaplin. I remember meeting Chaplin. Later we were placed in the Children's Aid Society Home. My brother and I remember playing outside there and seeing our father standing by a tree and watching us play. We saw him crying.

Even though Frank and Rose's native language was German, they were placed in English-speaking homes in Albany. In their eagerness to find foster homes for the children, the agents of the Children's Aid Society never hesitated to place a child in a home where his or her native language was not spoken. As the Cranor example illustrates, German-speaking children were placed in English-speaking homes; Italian, Slavic, and Scandinavian children were also placed in whatever homes could be found for them, no matter what language was spoken in the foster family.

Rose Cranor never saw her father again; she and her brother grew up in different families. Still, she had no regrets about coming to Missouri. She said of her orphan-train experience:

> I had a happy life with good foster parents, and a foster sister. Yet I have wondered what my life would have been had I stayed in New York with my parents. I would have had a completely different life. I have thought it strange how fate sets you up. And whatever fate gives you, that's what you've got.

Sydney Harvey Harley and his sister, Emily, also were fated to grow up in different families when they came to Centralia in 1910. Just as happened with Frank and Rose Cranor's father, Sydney and Emily Harvey's father could not both work and care for his children. Sydney explained the circumstances that resulted in their riding the orphan train:

> My father, who was a longshoreman, wanted to keep us, but simply couldn't provide a normal home. . . . Circumstances forced him to put us in the Children's Aid Society Home, because our mother abandoned the family shortly after we moved to New York City from England. He intended to come back for us, but when he finally did come to get us, Emily and I were on a trip headed for Missouri.

In Missouri, Sydney was taken by a dentist, Dr. S. E. Harley, and his wife, Mary. Emily was taken by Mary Harley's sister and brother-in-law. Living so near each other, Sydney and Emily were often together and had happy childhoods. Sydney said:

> I was very lucky. [The Harleys] had tried unsuccessfully for several years to have children. They had decided to adopt. When our train pulled into the station at Centralia, the Harleys were there waiting. . . . As they lined us up on the platform at the depot of the Wabash Station, we were all wondering about what would happen to us. Naturally, we all wanted to be adopted.

There were more than forty orphans on that train when it arrived at the Wabash depot in Centralia. Sydney, with tongue-in-cheek, said the reason the Harleys chose him was: "I was such a handsome young devil. . . . That's why they wanted me." In a more serious mood, Sydney said, "I was so lucky. . . . They chose me."

Sydney and Emily's father kept in touch with them through the Children's Aid Society and Mrs. Harley's letters. Thirty-two years after their father turned them over to the society, he came to see Sydney and Emily. Sydney said of that visit, "I just thought it was nice when I saw him. I appreciated the fact when he told us he really didn't intend to leave us."

Two brothers, Edward and Peter Newman, who came on one of the last of the orphan trains to Missouri in 1929, also were separated. When the train arrived in Trenton, Peter and Edward were taken by Mr. and Mrs. Dolph Smith. Peter was big enough to work on the farm, and when the Smiths decided they could not keep both children, they chose to keep Peter.

Edward was nine years old and small for his age. No one volunteered to take him, and the Reverend Mr. Swan was preparing to take him back to New York. As a last resort, Swan asked the Waddell family to take Edward on a trial basis. That home did not work out.

He was then placed with the Hatcher family. He enjoyed the Hatcher home because he had "lots of toys to play with." But he "hung around men who used foul language," so Swan removed him from the Hatcher's home.

Edward Newman is the third boy from the left in the front row in this photograph of the children in Tindall School in Grundy County in 1930. He came to Trenton in 1929 and was first placed with his brother, Peter, with a farm family near Trenton. They decided they could not keep two children, so Edward was temporarily placed in two other homes. Just before he was to be sent back to New York, another family sent word they wanted to see him. They thought he might be too small, but he promised them he would grow. He remained with the family until he established a home of his own. (Patrick-Sheets-Trickel Collection, Trenton, Mo.)

He was staying in the Old Plaza Theatre building waiting to return to New York when the W. D. Hack family of Tindall notified Swan they would take the boy on trial. He rode alone the four miles from Trenton to Tindall in a taxi. But when the Hacks saw him, they decided he was too small.

Faced with returning to an orphanage in New York, Edward Newman "sold himself" to the Hacks by saying, "I will grow." Mr. and Mrs. Hack took him at his word. He did grow and lived with the Hacks until he married in 1941.

Louis Vallieres Skidmore was separated from his sister, Rosalie. She had been taken to the Midwest on an orphan train ahead of her brother. He never saw her again.

When the orphan train that Louis rode on stopped in Skidmore, Missouri, in 1911, all the other children quickly found new homes. Only Louis was left on the platform at the end of the evening. Ella Skidmore, the young daughter of Mr. and Mrs. R. A. Skidmore, felt sorry for him because he had not found a foster family. She ran home and persuaded her mother to come back to meet him.

Mrs. Skidmore saw Louis and agreed to take him on a trial basis. He eventually became a permanent member of the Skidmore family although he was never legally adopted. Ella Skidmore was always proud that Louis was her foster brother.

Louis Vallieres Skidmore, who taught veterinary medicine at the University of Nebraska for thirty-eight years, came to Skidmore, Missouri, in 1911. All the children had been chosen except Louis, when a young girl, Ella Skidmore, persuaded her mother to take him. He grew up in Skidmore and graduated from the University of Missouri. In 1951 he went to New York and had a marker placed on his mother's grave. He never located his sister, Rosalie. (University of Missouri Archives)

As an adult, Louis tried on several occasions to find his biological sister, Rosalie, but he never succeeded. In remembrance, he named his daughter Rosalie.

Often large families were separated in the selection process of the orphan trains. The four Rifenburgh children are one example of this unfortunate practice.

In 1910 the Rifenburgh children arrived in Bowling Green,

Throughout its history, the Children's Aid Society separated brothers and sisters. Four Rifenburgh children were in a group that arrived in Lebanon, Missouri, in 1909 with chaperons Annie Laurie Hill and B. W. Tice. One of the boys, Nelson Ray, wrote: "Arriving in a strange town, being 'picked over' by prospective foster parents, words can't describe the terror, heartbreak and loneliness of being separated from sisters and brothers." Nelson Ray remembered that when the representative from the Children's Aid Society came for the children, his father put an ax over his shoulder and walked away into the woods. (Annette Riley Fry Papers, 1882–1983, Western Historical Manuscript Collection–Columbia)

Missouri. Howard Rifenburgh, not quite four years old, ran up to W. P. Darnell and said, "Mister, won't you take me?" Mr. and Mrs. Darnell had come to Bowling Green from their home in Curryville without even knowing what an orphan train was. They had no intention of taking an orphan that day, so they went away without Howard.

Later in the day, they decided they would take "the little fat boy if he were not already spoken for." With that, Howard Rifenburgh became a part of the Darnell family. He was the only one of the Rifenburgh children who did not have to change foster homes every few years and the only one who was legally adopted. The others moved from foster family to foster family every few years until they were adults.

Some orphan-train riders had a long journey together be-

Howard Rifenburgh was adopted by Mr. and Mrs. W. P. Darnell of Curryville, who had not intended to adopt an orphan. He was the only one of his family to be legally adopted, but he kept in touch with his brothers and sister. (Annette Riley Fry Papers, 1882–1983, Western Historical Manuscript Collection, Columbia, Mo.)

fore they reached Missouri and were separated from brothers or sisters. In 1918 a train had gone first to Texas and then made its way north to Missouri. Finally, it came to the whistle-stop of Pennsboro, Missouri, in Dade County.

Three children with the last name of Wilde were on that train. They were placed in the same town but in different homes. It was ten years before they found out they had lived near each other all that time. After that, they stayed in touch with one another. However, the three who came to Missouri never heard anything about their other nine or ten brothers and sisters. They never knew if they had remained with their biological parents, were placed in an orphanage, or came west on an orphan train.

On at least one occasion, however, the Reverend Mr. Swan could not bear to separate children from the same family. The twins, Dorothy and Susan Bond, had been placed in an orphanage in Brooklyn when they were six years old.

Contrary to most people's impressions of life in an orphans' home, the Bond twins enjoyed it. Susan Bond said in 1985, "Those were the happiest years of our lives. On every Saturday we went to the Brooklyn Bridge for a walk or to Coney Island. We then went home and had our usual meal, ginger snaps and milk."

They lived in the Brooklyn orphanage only two years. Then they were brought to Missouri on an orphan train. Susan remembered the day they left Brooklyn: "That day we were to leave Mr. Swan of Sedalia, Missouri, came after us. We were checked by a doctor, given a bath, new clothes, and both of us crying for we didn't want to leave. With Mr. Swan we went then to the train and cried all the way to Vandalia [Missouri]."

At Vandalia, the Bond twins and three other children got off the train with Swan. Together they went to the opera house. At first, different families wanted one of the twins, but not both. Swan refused to separate them. Susan Bond wrote: "They wanted to separate me and my sister but Mr.

Twins Dorothy and Susan Bond enjoyed their time at the orphanage and cried when they had to leave. Susan reported that they cried all the way to Vandalia and cried "during the whole *show*" as the children were selected by foster parents. The Reverend Mr. Swan insisted that the girls stay together. (Patrick-Sheets-Trickel Collection, Trenton, Mo.)

Swan would not allow [it]. Different people told me later that we both cried during the whole *show*."

Finally, a couple agreed to take them both, but the twins stayed with them for only a short time. Although Susan does not remember it, Swan decided that the placement was not suitable and moved them to another home.

They lived in the second home for fourteen years. Their placement there was not altogether successful. Susan wrote of their new parents: "I have no idea why our parents took us in for it was not a happy home. The husband's family never quite accepted us but our [foster] mother's family were wonderful people."

Like most of the orphan-train riders, the Bond twins felt the emotional pain of not knowing their biological parents and later tried to find them. Susan Bond wrote of their search:

> We tried for years to find out something about our family but all . . . we wrote knew nothing about Lulu Bond. In July 10, 1924, we had a letter from the Brooklyn Savings Bank that they had two accounts in that bank deposited by Lulu Bond—one in trust for Susan Bond and one in trust for Dorothy Bond. There was a lot of correspondence and finally in December 25, 1924 [we heard] from the Aid Society that Mr. E. H. Opitz worked hard for the money and persuaded the bank to turn [it] over to them. They enclosed a check for $36.44 for each of us. We wrote and thanked him for his trouble.

After receiving her inheritance of $36.44, Susan married Carl Schulz in 1924. In the years that followed, their two sons died at birth. She felt that perhaps with genetic information about her biological parents, her children might not have died.

SIX

Brothers and Friends

The Lawyers and the Jahnes

The experiences of the four Lawyer brothers reflect both the successes and the failures of the trains. The brothers were the sons of Harvey Andrew Lawyer, who was blind, and his wife, Loella. The Lawyers had been farmers living near Middleburg, New York. Then Loella Lawyer took the baby, Perry Paul, and left. Her family never heard from her again.

Harvey Lawyer tried to care for his children alone. He sent them to school, but they had only one coat and one pair of boots to share. Only one brother at a time could go to school in the wintertime.

Soon, their grandparents took over their care. Then in 1907 their grandfather died. Because of the blindness of their father and their grandmother's illness, the State of New York put them in an orphans' home.

Shortly after that, the Children's Aid Society took custody of the brothers. The society then sent the four brothers—Alclo, Noah, Stoddard Arthur, and James—on an orphan train to Missouri. Gus and John Jahne, who were also brothers, were on that same westbound train.

The trip was not easy. Years later Alclo told his wife, Gladys, he recalled the hard, stiff backs and seats on the train. There were "velvet-looking places" to sit or lie, but these actually were "very stickery like lying on pins."

The train ran day and night. The children were allowed to get off at some stops to run and play. Sometimes at the stops there were people to look them over and choose a child.

Finally, the Lawyer brothers arrived in Sedalia with several other children. The Reverend Mr. Swan then took the group to Savannah in Andrew County, Missouri. When the children arrived, the carload of boys and another carload of girls were taken to the courthouse by the Reverend Mr. and Mrs. Swan. They were presented to the prospective foster parents and curious citizens of the county.

According to Gus Jahne, there were thirty boys in one car of the train and probably about the same number of girls in another car. Most of the children were placed in and around Savannah.

The youngest of the group was Gus Jahne, who was between four and five. He was taken by a farm family almost immediately, along with his brother, John, who was eight or nine.

The Lawyer brothers experienced the agonies of not being among the first taken, but finally they were separated and went individually to different farm families.

According to Gladys Lawyer, Noah was the most fortunate of the four boys. He was taken by a well-known dairy farmer, who treated him like a son. He was renamed Robert, his foster father's first name, but later he took his own name back.

Alclo and James (Jim) Lawyer did not find permanent homes at first but were separated and moved from place to place. Both brothers were kept out of school to work as soon as the ground could be plowed in the spring.

Alclo suffered the further cruelty of being allowed only one serving of food, while the natural son of his foster father could have all the food he wanted. Alclo was often left at the table to watch the other boy eat.

An inspector of the Children's Aid Society, dressed as a farmer, visited the farm where Alclo had been placed. Thinking the inspector was from the area, Alclo's foster father complained that his foster son was "not much."

The inspector had already heard about the hard work, the missed school days, and the food limitations that Alclo had experienced. He moved Alclo to a new family.

The fourth Lawyer brother, Stoddard Arthur (Art), was placed in Andrew County with a mail carrier's family. There he was treated well. Gladys Lawyer says, "I remember he later took physical education at the YMCA and was well into body-building, and became a candidate for 'Mr. America.' "

Although they were placed in different homes and although Jim and Alclo Lawyer were moved to different families after placement, the four brothers and Gus and John Jahne stayed in touch with one another.

As Gladys recalls, Gus Jahne was often with Noah Lawyer and his wife, "visiting at my parents' home, where the man I married, Alclo Lawyer, was working and living." She also remembers that "Soon after Noah was married, he took his

Five-year-old Gus Jahne is seated in front beside his brother, John. In the back, Noah and James Atwell Lawyer are standing to the left with Walter and Herman Selle to the right. (Patrick-Sheets-Trickel Collection, Trenton, Mo.)

family back to New York, but they came back to visit every year."

When World War I came, Jim joined the navy and Alclo joined the army. After the war, Jim married and moved to Michigan where he owned a successful nightclub. Alclo and Gladys did not see him again until just before the reunion of the four brothers in the spring of 1965. Jim lived in Michigan until his death in the 1970s.

As many as three of the brothers were living in Andrew County at the same time. Still, it was not until 1965 that the four brothers got together as a family again. In the meantime all the brothers had married and established families of their own.

Alclo and Gladys were married in 1925 in Andrew County, where Alclo farmed. They later moved to St. Joseph were Alclo learned the construction business. For a while he and Art worked together for a tinner when both were living in St. Joseph.

Noah also married, but for a while he continued to work for the dairyman who had become his foster father. Gladys remembers, "We rode the milk wagon with Noah. All through the years we were very close, Noah and Alclo and [our] families. We had weekend ice cream parties at the dairyman's home. That place was always full of the boys who were sent to Andrew County [by the Children's Aid Society]. We almost forgot the slow, uncomfortable train ride. The four scared little boys had managed to keep friends with others who had been on the train." Art Lawyer lost touch with his brothers for sixteen years, but he renewed the contact with them in the 1960s.

Gladys Lawyer felt very close to the four orphan boys who had come to Andrew County. She said, "They all have been and still are my very life."

Noah and Art Lawyer told their own stories of their experiences. They remember very hard days in New York when the only clothes they had were sacks. They also remember hard days of labor on farms in Andrew County.

Noah's memories of his life on the dairy farm are not as pleasant as Gladys Lawyer's account makes it seem. He recalls that the dairy farmer had seven other orphan boys milking for him. His foster father often made him promises about the future that he did not keep. Noah sometimes ran away only to be lured back by more promises. He also recalls being abused and teased in school because he was an orphan. Eventually, he did leave his foster home to become a circus wrestler. A few years after he married, he moved back to New York.

Art also left his foster family as soon as he could. He became well known as an athlete while in high school. He believes he could have made the Olympic track team if he had not had a leg injury. Still, both Noah and Art agree that despite the hard work they experienced on the farms of their foster parents, they are thankful for the orphan trains. They believe that they probably would not have survived childhood if they had continued to live in New York.

The friendship between Gus and John Jahne and the Lawyer brothers continued throughout their lives.

Gus and his brother were lucky because they were not separated. They were placed with a farmer and his wife who had no children, Mr. and Mrs. Fred Karrasch. Their farm was not too far from the dairy farm where Noah Lawyer was placed.

John Jahne grew up on the Karrasch farm and married Ora Crawford in 1922. He taught in various northwestern Missouri rural schools, and in 1928 he received a B.S. degree from the University of Missouri. During the 1930s he served as educational adviser in the Civilian Conservation Corps at Kingman and Mount Vernon, Missouri, from 1934 to 1937. Later he was superintendent of schools at New Point, Pickering, Ravenwood, and Quitman, all in Missouri. In 1946 he received a master's degree from Drake University.

Gus Jahne married Sylvia Mowrey in June 1928 at the Savannah Baptist Church. Their son, Gary, was born in 1934. Gus worked at a variety of jobs, first for the telephone company as a cable splicer, then as a construction worker in St. Joseph. During World War II he was a light-tractor operator for the army. His last job before he retired was as a butcher in St. Joseph.

Both the Lawyer brothers and the Jahne brothers learned the value of hard work in their foster homes. These six Missourians, like many other orphan-train riders, made valuable contributions to their state and country.

SEVEN

The Weirs

A Family United, Separated, and Reunited

Dorothy Weir Davidson remembers questions about the placement of herself, her sister, and her brother in Trenton, Missouri, with the Woodruff family. She tells how she and her sister and brother were reunited, then separated because racial questions arose, and then united again. Scottie, or Billy as he was later called, was two, Dorothy was five, and Phyllis was seven.

> My brother came with a group of very young children before the train. How I do not know, but they called Mrs. Woodruff and said they had this little boy (two years old) [and he] needed to have a home for the night. She wasn't very interested, but she went and took a look and took him home for the night and that was all it took. They kept him.
>
> The Children's Aid Society knew Mr. and Mrs. Woodruff wanted a girl; so they wrote a letter to the Woodruffs that they had a little girl that was the sister to the boy they had, and would they be interested on a trial basis. They were and they sent her down.
>
> Later some way Mrs. Woodruff's sisters met Phyllis and Billy [Dorothy's brother and sister], and they thought Phyllis had colored blood in her, because of her dark coloring and flat nose. She was born without a bridge in her nose. With the seed of doubt in Mrs. Woodruff's mind, they [sent] Phyllis back to New York,

> but they missed her so much after having her for awhile they had Dr. Swan bring her back to Trenton. I think she was in New York about two weeks.

The letters exchanged between the Reverend Mr. Swan and the Woodruffs, who were both attorneys practicing in Trenton, give a full explanation of the Weir children's placement.

The first of these letters that still exists is dated October 11, 1930. It is from Swan, written from Sedalia: "Dear Friend. We were very sorry that we did not [have] time to talk with you longer at the depot concerning Phyllis. Mrs. Swan is planning to go east in a few days to return one of her girls. If you do not want to keep Phyllis let [us] know at once."

He then writes that he will pick up Phyllis from the Woodruffs. "I'll take [her] to meet Mrs. Swan. She will go from Omaha to Chicago. Would you be willing to pay Phyllis fare to Chicago? If so have her ready to put [on] the train as I go through Chillicothe. Wire as soon as you get this your decision. In haste, . . ."

Apparently the Woodruffs also replied in haste because by November 24, 1930, Swan in another letter apologizes for not answering sooner. (He spells Phyllis's name several ways in his letters about her.)

> Very Sorry that you have determined to give up Phylis. According to our promise we will remove her. Just what we can do with her we are at a loss to know. We will take the matter up immediately with the office & let you know as soon as we get a reply. Could you not make inquiry among your friends, perhaps some one would like to have her. If you know of a good home let her go & stay with them until we can hear from the office. . . . Mrs. Swan went to New York since we saw you. She would have taken Phillis with her if you had not decided to keep her at the time.

Sometime after this letter, Mrs. Woodruff sent a telegram to the society: "Return Phyllis Weir with Mrs. Swan and we will keep her for sure."

Helen Baxter, a supervisor for the Children's Aid Society, wrote to Mrs. Woodruff on December 23, 1930:

> Upon receipt of your telegram Saturday, Mrs. Swan started west with Phyllis and by now she must be reestablished in your home. I was glad that you felt you wanted her back because it will be so nice for the children to grow up together. I am afraid Phyllis' future would not have been anywhere near as happy had she not returned.
>
> It seemed only fair to ask you to pay for Phyllis' ticket east and back to you again. The cost of the two tickets amounts to $23.50.

The sentence in Swan's letter of November 24, 1930, "Just what we can do with her we are at a loss to know," and his question, "Could you not make inquiry among your friends, perhaps some one would like to have her" may have had some influence on the Woodruffs' decision to take Phyllis back.

Apparently, however, the prosperity of the Midwesterner was not as great as Brace had thought, at least not in 1931, at the height of the Great Depression. The Woodruffs wrote Helen Baxter asking if they could be allowed to delay the payment of $23.50 for Phyllis's tickets.

But by January 27, 1931, they were able to send the money requested. On January 29 Helen Baxter acknowledged the receipt of the check for the tickets. She wrote she felt "certain that all has worked out for the best" for both the Woodruffs and Phyllis.

Meanwhile, another of the Weir children had been facing difficulties.

Dorothy Weir, sometimes referred to as Dora, had been placed with another family in Trenton in 1929. The Reverend

Dorothy Weir, in a photograph taken at the Wingate home. (Patrick-Sheets-Trickel Collection, Trenton, Mo.)

Mr. Swan announced in the *Trenton Republican-Times* that "Dorothy Weir, 5, has been placed with Mr. and Mrs. William H. Wingate."

Dorothy remained with the Wingates until February 1931. Then Mrs. Wingate left her husband. William Wingate asked the Woodruffs to care for Dorothy until his wife came back. The Woodruffs wrote J. W. Swan about the situation on February 18, 1931.

> After talking with Mr. Wingate, and after several visits by Dorothy with us since your letter, we have decided, if it meets with your approval, that we want Dorothy, at least on trial. She is more than willing and the children too are anxious for her. She visited us yesterday afternoon staying for supper, and when Mr. Wingate came for her, she begged him to let her

> stay—she said she wanted to stay all the time. It was only after my telling her to get ready and go with her daddy, that she consented. Of course, she thinks all the world of her daddy, but as you stated in your letter, she needs a mother.
>
> We believe that it will be to the best interest of all that they be in the same home. Of course, we would want Dorothy on trial, although from the three visits she has made to us during the past two weeks, we have no doubt of her being satisfactory. . . . Of course, we have to consider the financial side of the matter—as far as the trouble concerned, that will amount to very little, as I find Billy and Phyllis no trouble at all. Of course, Phyllis practically cares for herself and does a lot for us too, and is so willing. Dorothy seems to be just as nice a child as Billy and Phyllis and we are very anxious for her.
>
> If the above application meets with your approval, kindly send word to Mr. Wingate to turn her over to us, which I think he will take very kindly from his talk with us, or if you think necessary, you might come yourself and make the change.

The Swans replied on the following day, surprised but pleased that the Woodruffs wanted to take Dorothy.

> I cannot conceive a more noble thing to do than open your home and hearts to 3 lovely bro.-sister whose little hearts are longing for a mother & Father's love. I would understand that is a Christian act. The very thought that they can be in the same home with same environments, the same future out-look. I'll write Mr. Wingate to let you take Dorothy on trial, until I can come to Trenton & take the matter up with you. I'll be in no hurry to come to Trenton. You have our most earnest prayers for you and the children's success.

On February 23, 1931, the Woodruffs wrote Swan with more information about the reason the Wingates were giving Dorothy up. She apparently had become a pawn in the

Wingates' marital problems. The letter reflects how anxious the Woodruffs were about Dorothy and the Wingates' marital situation. It also reveals the pleasure they felt in reuniting the three siblings.

> We received your letter, Mr. Wingate asked us to take Dorothy for awhile in order that he might write his wife that Dorothy had been taken away—in an effort to get his wife back, he felt perhaps the jolt might bring her to her senses.
>
> I never saw anyone more devoted to a child, and more interested. He asked that [she] be allowed to go to her own school over near his store. Of course, we were glad to do this for him, and know it will meet with your approval; also we can kill two birds with one stone. We can try Dorothy. . . . [She] calls Mr. Woodruff "daddy" although [we] did not intend she should inasmuch if Mr. Wingate is able to take her back, . . . it might be hard to draw her away from us, and especially away from the children. She surely does enjoy her sister, Phyllis and [brother] Scottie. It is certainly a pleasure to have her and I am really in hope in many ways that everything works out so we can keep her although I feel that Wingates have first thought if he can arrange it. I am sure he will give her a good education and give everything possible for her.
>
> Dorothy is such an attractive child and seems to mind nicely so far. I have no trouble with her at all.

By March 12, 1931, Mrs. Woodruff wrote Swan again, "We received your letter a few days ago in regard to Dorothy. I believe that Mr. Wingate realizes that Mrs. Wingate will not return to him, as he stated he had a letter in which she refused to return—Mr. Wingate saying she was as mad as ever."

However, their awareness of the Wingates' problems did not cause the Woodruffs to make a definite decision about keeping Dorothy. In the next paragraph of the letter Mrs. Woodruff wrote: "We still have Dorothy and as yet have not made up our minds as to whether we can keep her. She undoubtedly is a lovely child and very obedient, and gets along nicely with the children."

Perhaps Mrs. Woodruff's doubts about keeping Dorothy were the result of the still uncertain status of the Wingates' marriage. But the Great Depression also may have been an important factor, as it had placed economic burdens on all families. Mrs. Woodruff's phrase, "whether we can keep her," may be about the economic situation of the time.

The letter also reveals for the first time that Dorothy is suffering from some sort of skin condition. Mrs. Woodruff describes it as an infection on different parts of her body and fingers. She feared the infection would spread to her other children. But she rested easy when the doctor assured her Dorothy would be all right in three or four days.

By March 16 the Woodruffs wrote Swan that Dorothy's skin condition had cleared up and they had decided to keep her with them. Swan's letter of March 18 offered advice:

> I have written Mr. Wingate to turn Dora over to you. You would be responsible for her. Do not believe Mrs. W. will return to live with him. When you study carefully the dispositions of the 3 you will find them not similar in every thing. May have to deal differently with each in training them. Wishing you abundant success, may you both receive Wisdom from whom Wisdom is promised, "If any man lack wisdom Let him ask Him who is all Wisdom."

Sometime later the Woodruffs decided to take Dorothy on a permanent basis. They concluded that much of her nervousness was caused by conflict between her feelings for them and her feelings for her first foster father.

In an undated letter, using their law office letterhead, they wrote to Mrs. R. G. Neal, a visitor for the society, that they felt it would be better if Mr. Wingate did not see Dorothy anymore.

> If you will remember when we first took Dorothy, you said to me in Mr. Wingate's store that of course Mr. Wingate would like to see Dorothy at times and I said it would be all right with me.
>
> Dorothy has been on a terrible nervous strain, is unable to go to sleep at nights for hours and I had no idea the cause. Today, she came home from school after Mr. Wingate had seen her and gave her some candy, and she had a nervous collapse and was unable to go to school. She also stated she was nervous in school and that her stomach "jumped,"—jerked, I think she meant.

The Woodruffs' letters give some insight into the emotional conflicts many of the orphan-train children must have felt, especially when they were moved several times. From the evidence in the letters, the stress of leaving the Wingates and the hesitancy of the Woodruffs in taking her must have been very hard for Dorothy and may have caused some of her physical and other problems.

Another undated letter from the Woodruffs, apparently written sometime after October 31, 1931, after J. W. Swan's retirement, shows the pride the Woodruffs had begun to take in the children.

> Dear Mr. Swan:
>
> Have been intending writing you for sometime inasmuch as we received a letter from the Children's Aid Society on October 31st stating that the Methodist Home for Children, St. Louis, had recently taken over the supervision of their Missouri children and, as I understand from the letter, Miss Georgia Greenleaf, Box 323, Jefferson City, Missouri, was their Field Secretary now.
>
> If this means that you are no longer our "Grandpa" we want to say here and now we don't like it. In fact, we didn't like the job at all of telling the children but they were real sweet about it. When I told them that perhaps you would not call and see us for the Society, Billy said, "well, anyway, he is still our Grandpa."

We really do feel like we had lost some of our family. Everyone of us always enjoyed your visits so much and so often when we had something to eat which the children enjoyed, one would remark that we ought to save it until Grandpa came. So you see how it is here.

We all have certainly enjoyed our association and pleasant relations with you and Mrs. Swan, and surely hope we shall have the pleasure of meeting you both again. Anytime you happen to be through here, don't fail to call on us.

The children are all fine—enjoying a Thanksgiving vacation. Phyllis and Dorothy are both taking violin in the school here and are considered quite talented. Billy, of course, is still in kindergarten and thinks he should have a horn to blow. He has high aspirations of being a member of the band at sometime. With best wishes to you both from all, we are

Yours very truly,
WOODRUFF & WOODRUFF,

Billy insisted that I read over this letter for him, which I did and then he insists that I add for him "Sweet Grandpa Swan."

Perhaps this change in the supervision of the children and Swan's answer on December 5 caused the Woodruffs to decide to adopt the children legally. Swan wrote,

Dear Friends. We thank you very much for your kind letter. The 22nd Oct I passed my 80 milestone. Mrs. Swan and I resigned. Now I am a man of leisure good for nothing. We greatly appreciate the fact that we met you & tried to interest you in our dear children. You assumed a great responsibility in taking the 3 dear ones. We believe you have laid by some treasure in heaven & trust the *Jewels* will greatly reward you. Mrs. Swan sends her congratulations to you and the children. Tell Billy . . . we are still grandma & grandpa.

By 1932 the Woodruffs had started proceedings to legally adopt all three children. Mrs. Woodruff wrote the Children's

The Reverend Mr. and Mrs. Swan with their grandchildren. (Patrick-Sheets-Trickel Collection, Trenton, Mo.)

Aid Society about their plans. On September 8, Helen Baxter wrote saying she was asking Georgia Greenleaf to write a letter of recommendation. Once she received the letter, she would be delighted to approve the adoption.

The letter of recommendation from Georgia Greenleaf must have arrived in New York City very quickly. Only fifteen days later Helen Baxter wrote telling the Woodruffs that the adoption papers were being sent by registered mail.

Despite the speed of Helen Baxter's reply, the legal papers did not arrive in time for filing in the November session of the Grundy County Court. However, they were ready for the February 1933 session. Then Dorothy, Phyllis, and Billy Weir were reunited for good.

Phyllis, who had been sent back to New York City and then returned at the Woodruffs' request, was singled out in the Woodruffs' March 6, 1933, letter to the society announcing the adoption. Mrs. Woodruff called her "the little 'flat nose' one [who] is the pride of our heart and so happy."

However, the three Weir children in Missouri had yet another brother. They were not reunited with him until they were adults, though. Eddie Weir had not come on an orphan train to Missouri. Instead he had been taken by his grandparents, Mr. and Mrs. Ephram Rabideau, of Glenelm, Quebec. Eddie had traced his brother and sisters to Mexico, Missouri, after they had moved with their adoptive parents. He came from his home in Quebec to see them.

From earlier correspondence with Eddie and from their reunion with him, Billy, Phyllis, and Dorothy learned that their mother had died in 1928. Their father had gone to live in Canada after the younger children had been placed with the Children's Aid Society. By the time of the reunion, Mr. and Mrs. Woodruff had died, so Eddie never had a chance to meet the two people who had done so much to reunite his brother and sisters.

But Eddie Weir had never forgotten his brother and two sisters. He named three of his children Bill, Dorothy, and Phyllis. The lifelong dream of the Weir children to be reunited occurred thirty-two years after their separation.

EIGHT

The Orphan-Train Legacy

The western-emigration policy of the Children's Aid Society had successes and failures. Sometimes the children and their foster parents were not suited to one another. There were instances of child abuse and neglect. Sometimes the children were overworked and did not have enough food. Often these children suffered the pain of separation from the only family they had ever known—their brothers and sisters.

Still, there were instances of generosity and love. Opportunities for family life and education made the policy successful for many of the orphan-train riders.

However, it is neither the numbers of the children placed in foster homes nor the claim the policy was an inexpensive way of solving juvenile crime that made the orphan trains successful. Their primary success was that those involved in child welfare became more aware of the importance of foster families.

The Children's Aid Society of New York did much to end the orphan-home system and defeat what Brace called the "asylum party." To him, people who believed in placing children in orphan asylums cared more about buildings and costs than children.

Of course, studies of childhood development would have eventually caused those who cared for orphans to recognize the value of Brace's ideas. But the western-emigration policy of the Children's Aid Society was the first to bring about extensive foster-home placement.

Mamie Harmisch Curn Murray came to Missouri in 1911. The doll was given to her in New York by a wealthy supporter of the Children's Aid Society when she was taken to his home. The people who adopted her in Missouri were "wonderful parents," but she longed all her life to know someone from her own family. (Annette Riley Fry Papers, 1882–1983, Western Historical Manuscript Collection–Columbia)

Nevertheless, Brace's plan had two sides to it. While arguing the importance of family environment for orphans, he was, more often than not, separating children of the same family.

The legacy of the orphan trains is also their influence on attitudes toward orphans. Some Midwestern states expressed fear of the culturally, racially, and socially unidentified children who came on the trains. Because of this, Missouri and other states passed laws against the importation of children.

Most adults who came in contact with these children came to know them as individuals, not as types. They realized the orphan-train riders had emotional and personal needs, just as they themselves had.

Further, for those who became part of the orphans' families as foster parents, brothers, sisters, husbands, and wives, the experience was a shaping influence in their lives. As

Gladys Lawyer said about her husband, Alclo Lawyer, and the other three Lawyer brothers, "They all have been and still are my very life."

People of small Missouri towns such as Lebanon took pride in their role in aiding the orphans. Even today the orphan trains are very much a part of the culture and history of many Missouri towns. A front-page announcement in the *Lebanon Republican* reported with satisfaction on January 7, 1910: "The local committee . . . had received about seventy-five applications for children, hence there was no difficulty in securing satisfactory homes for the twelve brought here. The children were exceptionally bright and attractive, ranging in age from 2 1/2 years to 15 years." Today those residents of Lebanon who remember the trains feel proud their town played a role in solving this problem.

The success of the trains also can be demonstrated by the fact that they were imitated by other institutions, cities, and countries. The first imitator, with the modification that all the children had to be placed before they left the city, was the Catholic New York Foundling Hospital.

In Boston three organizations—the New England Home for Little Wanderers, the Home for Destitute Catholic Children, and the Children's Mission—placed thousands of children, many of them in the Midwest.

A recent example of placement of children was the policy of the British government following World War II, when more than two thousand orphans were sent to foster homes in Australia. Unlike the orphan-train riders we have interviewed, whose grief may have been overcome by time, many of the English children were bitter about their experiences. A series of two articles by Sue Adler appeared in the *Observer* (London) on July 19 and 26, 1987.

Shirley Ronge, sent from one of the Dr. Barnardo orphan homes in England when she was eleven, says that being sent to Australia "was the worst thing they ever did, sending me out there. I know that I agreed, but a child of that age should not be asked that sort of question, because they do

Henry Lee Jost became one of Missouri's orphan-train success stories. He was taken in by a judge in Nodaway County and later apprenticed to a farmer. At age fifteen he hired himself out as a farmhand until he had earned enough to study law. He served as prosecuting attorney in Jackson County, as mayor of Kansas City for two terms, and in the U.S. Congress. (Annette Riley Fry Papers, 1882–1983, Western Historical Manuscript Collection–Columbia)

not know what is involved. From the day I arrived, I can honestly say that all I wanted was to come back to England." Syd Stephenson states, "I have never forgiven Britain for deserting us." George Wilkins, now a millionaire, says of his placement home, it was a "place totally without love."

The English children share with the U.S. orphan-train riders the emptiness of not knowing their biological families. Sandra Bennett, a nurse in Sydney, still longs to find out "who she is." Others, such as Harold Haig, have been reunited with their brothers or sisters, just as U.S. orphans sometimes were.

The separation of children from the same family, as frequently happened to U.S. children, was, according to Sue Adler, "one particularly callous aspect of the migration schemes. The policy of exporting Britain's unwanted children to a continent 13,000 miles away will always remain a shameful chapter in Britain's social history."

Perhaps because the orphan-train riders were not shipped overseas, or perhaps because the orphan trains are in the more distant past, or perhaps because Americans tend to accept practical solutions to social problems, most probably do not consider the western-emigration policy of the Children's Aid Society and the Mercy Trains of the New York Foundling Hospital "shameful chapters" in the history of the United States. For those who rode the trains and their relatives and descendants, their experiences may contain painful memories. Still, these experiences also contain the seeds for many success stories.

The family lore of the orphan-train riders shows that the hardships, hard work, and determination of many orphans enabled them to develop into model citizens with strong family ties. Their experience fulfills the American dream that people can achieve anything they want through hard work, despite ancestry or environment.

FOR MORE READING

Children West: A History of the Placing Out System of the New York Children's Aid Society 1853–1890, by Miriam A. Langsam (Madison: State Historical Society of Wisconsin, 1964), gives particular attention to the statistics of the Children's Aid Society and the methods of financing the trains.

The Dangerous Classes of New York and Twenty Years Work among Them, by Charles Loring Brace (Montclair, N.J.: Patterson Smith, 1967), is the autobiographical account of Brace's work at the society and the beginning of the orphan trains.

"It Took Trains to Put Street Kids on the Right Track," by Donald Dale Jackson (*Smithsonian Magazine* [August 1986]: 95–103), uses the research of Michael Patrick, Evelyn Sheets, and Evelyn Trickel as a basis for an account of the orphan trains.

"I Was on the Orphan Train," by Henrietta Wiens (*The Plain Truth* 49 [April 1984]: 31–32 and 43), is an eyewitness account written in adulthood by one of the orphan-train riders.

The Life of Charles Loring Brace, by Emma Brace (New York: Ayers, 1976), is Brace's daughter's story of her family's involvement in the orphan trains.

New York Street Kids, by John Van Hartz (New York: Dover, 1978), presents graphically the experiences of street children, the so-called street arabs.

"Not Wanted," by Joseph Israels II (*Saturday Evening Post* [December 18, 1948]: 90–95), recounts the emotions the children felt as they took part in the western-emigration policy (the orphan trains) of the Children's Aid Society.

Orphan Train: A Novel, by James Magnuson and Dorothea Petrie (New York: Dover, 1978), dramatizes the love between a woman who accompanies children west and a photographer in a highly fictionalized account of the first orphan train.

Orphan Trains, by Annette Riley Fry (New York: New Discovery Books, 1994), presents the orphan-train experience with photographs, illustrations, and a brief text.

"The Orphan Trains," by Leslie Wheeler (*American History Illustrated* [December 1983]: 10–23), is a historical account of the orphan trains using previously published sources.

The Orphan Trains: Placing Out in America, by Marilyn Holt (Lincoln: University of Nebraska Press, 1992) is a history of the orphan trains using sources that are not always clearly credited.

"Sentimental Journey: Children of the Orphan Trains," by Rachel Lemonine (*Louisiana Life* [May–June 1985]: 56–62), emphasizes the personal experiences of some of those who rode the orphan trains.

We Are a Part of History: The Story of the Orphan Trains, by Michael Patrick, Evelyn Sheets, and Evelyn Trickel (Virginia Beach: Donning, 1994), draws upon published accounts, unpublished documents, and interviews with surviving orphan-train riders to document the family histories of some orphans.

"When Orphans Went West for a Home," by George DeWan (*Newsday* part 2 [June 22, 1983]: 4–5), is a brief historical account of the operation of the orphan trains.

For More Information

Orphan Train Heritage Society of America, Inc.
614 East Emma Avenue, No. 115
Springdale, AR 72764
(501) 756-2780
Hours: 8 A.M.–1 P.M Monday–Friday or by appointment.

INDEX

ABOUT THE AUTHORS

Michael Patrick, a native of Missouri, is a graduate of Southern Illinois University and the University of Missouri–Columbia. He taught English literature and folklore at the University of Missouri–Rolla for more than twenty-five years and presently teaches folklore at the University of Southern Alabama in Fairhope. (photo by Sam Griffin, courtesy University Relations, University of Missouri)

Evelyn Trickel is a native of Grundy County, Missouri. She graduated from the University of Missouri–Columbia and Central Missouri State University and teaches an Elderhostel course on the orphan trains at North Central Missouri College in Trenton. In 1996 she received the Charles Loring Brace Award from the Orphan Train Heritage Society of America for her many contributions to orphan-train research.

9 780826 211217